P9-DBY-505

the art and craft of
jewelry

janet fitch

photography by kevin summers

GROVE PRESS
NEW YORK

To my family and Martin Somervail

Edited and designed by
Mitchell Beazley International Ltd
Michelin House, 81 Fulham Road,
London SW3 6RB

Design Director **Jacqui Small**
Executive Editor **Judith More**
Art Editor **Trinity Fry**
Editor **Catherine Smith**
Production **Sarah Schuman**
Photography by **Kevin Summers**
Illustrations by **Michael Hill**

Copyright (c) Mitchell Beazley International Ltd 1992
All rights reserved. No part of this work may be reproduced or utilized in any form or by any means, electronic or mechanical, including photocopying, recording or by any information storage and retrieval system, without the prior written permission of the publishers.

Reprinted 1992, 1993
Published by Grove Press
A division of Grove Press, Inc.
841 Broadway
New York, NY 10003-4793

Published in Canada by General Publishing Company, Ltd.

Note: The jewelry designs shown in this book are the copyright of the individual artists and may not be copied for commercial use.

Library of Congress Cataloging-in-Publication Data
Fitch, Janet
     The art and craft of jewelry / Janet Fitch,
        p.   cm.
     ISBN 0-8021-1464-4
     1. Jewelry making.   I. Title
TT212.F58 1992
745.594'2 - - dc20   91-45416
                                                            CIP

The publishers have made every effort to ensure that all instructions given in this book are accurate and safe, but they cannot accept liability for any resulting injury, damage or loss to either person or property whether direct or consequential and howsoever arising. The author and publishers will be grateful for any information which will assist them in keeping future editions up to date. British spellings have been retained throughout the text of the U.S. edition.

Typeset in Caslon No. 540 Roman 9.5/13pt and Gill sans Roman 9/13 pt. by Litho Link Ltd, Welshpool, Powys, Wales
Colour reproduction by Scantrans Pte Ltd, Singapore
Produced by Mandarin Offset
Printed and bound in Hong Kong
10 9 8 7 6 5 4 3 2 1

Page 1: This unique, hand-turned bangle is crafted from elm wood. The natural knots in the burr wood's surface produce a beautiful relief texture which the designer has emphasized by polishing and buffing with beeswax. The wood is also finished with Danish oil to seal it and enhance its natural colour. (Hayley Smith)

Previous page: Paper is a highly versatile jewellery material and can be manipulated to imitate the qualities of many other elements. This jagged bangle was fashioned by layering papier mâché around a twisted coathanger wire skeleton. The piece was left to dry, coated with layers of gold leaf and then polished. (Holli Hallett-Sullivan)

Opposite: A spandex bracelet can be embellished with assorted glass and plastic beads to give it interest and individuality. The faceted glass beads, quirky flower shapes and painted ceramic beads that decorate this elasticated cuff have been collected from all over the world. (Lil Gardner)

Overleaf left to right: Twisted silver wire earring and blue marble earring (Mary Farrell); interlinked watch face bracelet and spoon brooch with embedded found objects (John Wind); sequin charm bracelet (Laura Lee); glass eye brooch (Martin Somervail); hand-painted papier mâché brooch (Marion Elliot); brass cuff with enamel motifs (Maura Nicholson); glass earring bound with silver wire (Peter Foster); earring of linked gold-plated shapes with suspended hand-blown glass shape (Van der Straeten); brass, turquoise and shell dangle earring (Maura Nicholson); raw fleece button earring (Victoria Brown); polished and stained almond stone necklace (Eric Beamon); black and gold fleece bead bracelet (Victoria Brown); hand-painted wooden brooch (Annie Sherburne); paisley-shaped brooch with found objects embedded in resin (John Wind); starburst wire cuff (Mary Farrell); spandex charm bracelet (Eric Beamon); aluminium tubing and found glass brooch (Peter Foster).

contents

Compare the vanguard of post-modern jewellery design with the traditional history of the craft and you will find that they have little in common. What could creations like Simon Costin's rabbit skull designs (see p.17), Andrew Logan's mirror and resin pieces (see p.44), Louise Slater's acrylic and pebble brooches (see p.122) or Katherine Wilkins' driftwood pendants (see p.133) share with the elaborate gold filigree and *cloisonné* work, set with glittering rose-cut diamonds and rubies, which represents the pinnacle of Western jewellery production over the last 500 years and more? However, as archaeological finds have revealed, man's first jewellery was the teeth and claws of his prey, strung on natural fibre; ornaments which look strikingly modern. The pieces worn in the caves of the hunter-gatherers are the first link in a chain stretching across 40,000 years, which joins the works of art on these pages with rich and varied traditions of jewellery design that run back through time and across the cultures of the world.

The history of conventional jewellery is a tale of gold, silver and precious stones; a succession of collars, crowns, suites and tiaras made for kings and nobles. But there is another, parallel history of decorative objects worn by a wider cross-section of peoples across the globe. Folk, costume, ethnic and modern designer jewellery are all part of this alternative history, where ornament knows no rules.

The enormous vocabulary of materials used in so-called ethnic jewellery, dwarfs that of European jewellery and was a massive liberating force in 20th-century design. Africa exerted by far the greatest impact; unlike the Europeans, the Africans and many Asian peoples never lost sight of the prehistoric organic tradition. Bone (human and animal) wood, shell, roots, seeds and nuts are still used for beads. In Northern Nigeria, straw is used as earrings, and among the Bashima people straw is woven into bracelets and arm-bands. After the colonization of Africa, "found" European coins were worn as hair ornaments and attached to necklaces. While in the Americas, tropical feathers were used for necklaces and head-dresses by the Precolumbian civilization, North American Indians and Amazon tribes.

Ethnic jewellery shows a far bolder use of colour and contrasting materials than was dared in Europe before Modernism. Precious stones, glass beads, rough-hewn coral, bone and incised silver-work may all feature in the same piece, bringing with them clashes of turquoise, cream, pink, gleaming silver and other colours.

Since ancient times, Indian jewellers have supplied the demand for inexpensive jewellery. Bangles are made from conch shell, glass, iron and from the insect resin known as "Lac". Indian and East Asian jewellery is perhaps unique in the world for having incorporated sound into the aesthetic – bells are used extensively.

Ethnic jewellery does not exclude precious materials. Most non-European cultures have produced, and still are producing, sophisticated and intricate gold-work to rival the most skilled craftsmen of Europe. Yet at the same time, ethnic jewellers appreciated rougher finishes on their precious metals. The Fulani people of Mali produced massive round earrings by simply

Previous pages: An unusual collection of hand-coiled copper wire earrings. The burnished finish is achieved by placing each piece in an oxidizing solution.
(Caroline Coyne)

Overleaf (left to right): North Indian amber, coral and aluminium three-tiered necklace; red fabric and yellow metal necklace from Tibet; white metal hair combs from China; Zuni bracelet from North America; African glass trading bead necklace; yellow metal bead necklace from Ethiopia; Mexican white metal and bead earrings; Indian white metal ankle bracelet with red and green stones; metal bangle from Morocco; ancient Egyptian beads; 1960s enamelled scarab bracelets from a Cairo flea market; white metal and glass heart ring from India; 1950s bronze rings from Mali.

introduction

beating the gold into shape while the Precolumbians created stunning silhouettes of birds and monsters in beaten gold to use as earrings and other ornaments. And iron and copper wire is coiled into torques and armbands by the people of Eastern and Southern Africa, or wound around a central core of plant fibres to act as a bracelet. These basic finishes are now influencing Western jewellers like Van der Straeten (see p.93).

Primitive man

Since the beginning of mankind, vanity, humility, status, religion and superstition have all prompted the desire to embellish the human body. The social standing of primitive man was determined by the adornment of bones, feathers, teeth and claws; as byproducts of food. They represented his skill as a hunter. Pin-like clasps, fashioned from bone splinters, were also an integral part of a cave-dweller's wardrobe, securing the animal skins that kept the owner warm.

The earliest known jewellery was discovered at La Quina in France, where a hoard of beads made from animal teeth and bones was uncovered. These were ostensibly sported as pendants by Neanderthal man about 40,000 years ago. The very first jewellery was probably a garland of flowers and fruit. Although no traces of these primeval jewels have been left, the most enduring jewellery theme across continents and centuries is the representation of flowers and fruit.

Primitive jewellery was organic and emphasized the natural qualities and shapes of found objects. The materials used depended on what was available locally and on the lifestyle of the makers. The discovery of most of these pieces near burial sites suggests that they had both a supernatural and a social function.

The early traders

By the seventh millennium BC, jewellery was part of the international trading culture between the Mediterranean and the early mountain civilizations of Western Asia. Beads of Mediterranean coral have been discovered in the Neolithic city of Çatal Hüyük. By the fourth and third millennia BC, jewellery had become a complex part of complex civilizations; extraordinary strings of precious stones have been unearthed at the Royal Sumerian graves.

Quantities of glass beads have been discovered in the Caucasus and in the area ruled by the Mesopotamian civilization in the third millennium BC. Another type of ornamentation worn by Mesopotamians was the amulet; small, carved stone animals – doves, rams, birds and frogs – with a supernatural or spiritual value. Around the same time the Naqada civilization of Upper Egypt exploited steatite, one of the earliest composite materials for jewellery. It is a soft, easily carved stone with a soapy feel (hence it's name).

The ancient world

The Egyptians produced heavy, ornate choker-like collars encrusted with stones and head-dresses to wear over wigs. Because the methods involved were laborious and the pieces cumbersome, as an alternative, for ceremonial rituals, jewellery was conjured from natural resources and included collars of flowers, berries and olive leaves. Dedicated followers of fashion boasted ornaments crafted from organic materials like ivory, bone and gold, in addition to faience and enamels.

As well as the jewellers who made the massive sculptural gold jewellery with its lavish use of gemstones, uncovered in the tombs of the pharaohs, a second jewellery economy catered for the middle and lower orders. Beads were made from glass and a glazed pottery known as faience.

Throughout antiquity, from the Egyptian to the Mycenaean and finally Roman civilizations, coloured glass was adopted as a substitute for pearls, emeralds, turquoise and other precious stones. Antique fake pearls were constructed with glass beads backed by a thin piece of gold or silver foil – a technique which has continued more or less until the present day. Faience beads were mass-produced and coloured to imitate precious stones such as turquoise or lapis lazuli. Some faience necklaces have been found which represent, in miniature, floral garlands. A wall painting from the tomb of Sobkhatpe at Thebes depicts a goldsmith working alongside a hard-bead worker. It appears that in ancient times precious metal and gemstone pieces and nonprecious craft jewellery were produced by the same workshops, as in the 20th century, where firms design and manufacture both real and costume jewellery.

In Europe and Western Asia during the second and first millennia BC, jewellery reflected the advances of the Bronze and Iron Ages. Brooches, bangles and dresspins were simple geometric shapes – the hoop or disc – and featured abstract leaf or floral designs. The decoration could include inlaid enamel-like glass paste panels. In the British Isles, the Celts achieved a high standard of craftsmanship in gold and metals.

The Ancient Greeks and Etruscans were great innovators in design and execution and produced meticulously crafted granulated, filigree and enamelled jewellery, while the Romans were not so much innovators as perfectors of the techniques inherited from their predecessors. As a legacy of Rome's many conquests, the empire absorbed foreign influences and became a melting pot of craft and culture. Legions returned to Rome with the plunders of their conquests and brought enslaved craftsmen to impart their knowledge to young Roman apprentices. They also introduced emeralds and developed the skill of cutting and engraving gems. As the Roman Empire crumbled, the Barbarians brought German and late Imperial fashions across Europe. These concentrated, technically, on extravagant high-relief creations in gold and silver and, thematically, on zoomorphic ornament. But for the next millennium of European history, jewellery was almost exclusively defined by cast and carved metals and set stones. In other parts of the world a vast array of materials continued to be used, but in Europe the jeweller's vocabulary shrunk rapidly with the spread of antique civilization and metal-working technology.

From the Middle Ages to the Renaissance

There are some isolated examples of European craft jewellery before the 18th century. Popular jewellery in the Middle Ages consisted of brooches or badges commemorating pilgrimages. Usually cast in lead, these depicted the face of the saint or an image of the shrine.

From the 11th century, Venice became the focal point for the manufacture of glass and fine jewellery. The Venetians injected elegance and grace into their designs, which heavily influenced the rest of Europe. Because of the popularity of their precious designs, demand exceeded supply and so craftsmen produced cut paste, European jewellery was worn overwhelmingly by Royal families and their courtiers and was cast in precious or semi-precious materials.

With the advent of the Renaissance, jewellery design was totally rejuvenated by the influence of themes from classical antiquity and mythological and allegorical figures influenced pendants and brooches. This era brought in an explosion of elaborate gold, pearls, enamels and magnificent gems.

The 17th and 18th centuries

The 17th century saw a refreshing transition from gaudy excess to jewellery that underlined the status of the diamonds. Crucial to the development of paste were the developments in the technology of glass-cutting and manufacture. In the late 17th century, a deposit of natural crystal discovered near Bristol, England, was found to be suitable for paste jewellery in imitation of rose-cut diamonds. At the same time, an English manufacturer produced the first glass compound which could convincingly imitate diamonds. It was cut from flint glass produced with lead oxide. By 1740, the finest paste stones cut from English glass were being produced in Paris by Georges-Frederic Stras. Glass pastes were adopted by the highest in society as well as by

facsimiles of real gems for people with lesser budgets.

At the Tudor court in England, the first marriage of fine artist and jeweller took place with Nicholas Hilliard's collaboration with jewellers on the design of miniature portraits in jewelled cases. The Italian Renaissance also produced items designed by artist-designers, such as that of Cellini. During the later Middle Ages, Venice and Milan became the main world sources for quality "paste" jewellery made from coloured glass. But until the growth of the middle classes from the 17th century onward, and the concurrent technological advances in sophisticated; the genuine merits of jewellery as a fashion accessory became apparent and people began to appreciate tasteful design. In the 17th century, the development of diamond-cutting was in its infancy; by the 18th century, diamond-cutting had become a sophisticated craft and indeed the methods involved have altered comparatively little since.

Each age has invented its own definition of costume jewellery. In Europe, the 18th century ushered in an era of cut, glittering paste-set jewellery which has lasted until the present day, emulating the glitter of rose-cut fashionable ladies of lower status. Stras was appointed jeweller to Louis XV, King of France; arguably a recognition of the new artistic leadership of paste over precious jewellery.

Although paste work was strongly imitative of real jewels, the material had qualities which gave jewellers greater creative freedom than precious stones. Because it was softer, it could be cut into any shape, thereby allowing mosaic-style or pavé-set arrangements which were impossible to achieve at the time with precious stones. In addition, much larger stones could be set.

Developments in paste materials continued; by the 1780s, glass-makers could produce convincing glass imitations of opal.

The 18th century also saw discoveries of imitation gold metals. In 1720, the watch-maker Christopher Pinchbeck devised a golden alloy of copper and zinc. In Paris in 1785, copper was coated with gold and christened "pomponne". Other alloys imitating gold were known as "l'or de Mannheim", "Tombac" and "Simulor". The most interesting 18th-century jewellery was made in the materials of the industrial revolution – iron and steel. Decorative steel jewellery

cameos in jewellery led to the production of Wedgwood's remarkable tiny jasparware cameos set on steel necklaces, bracelets and other jewels. English steel jewellery was arguably the first non-precious jewellery produced in Europe since the Dark Ages which did not imitate fine precious stone and metal pieces.

Meanwhile, in 19th-century Berlin, a parallel ironwork jewellery industry emerged. Iron jewellery featuring cameos was in demand in Germany too, but Berlin's industry was remarkable chiefly for lightweight, feathery, lacy effects and the dark quality of the iron's colouring (which was often lacquered black).

brought different motifs to the fore – from insects to anchors, floral sprays to quivers of arrows. Events began to inspire jewellers – for example, the 19th-century archaeological finds at Herculaneum and Pompeii led to imitation classical styles.

The inventive, avant-garde nature of 20th-century jewellery was presaged on the fringes of 19th-century popular jewellery with the arrival of esoteric, humorous "conversation" jewels – pieces which were intended not so much to make their owner look glamorous as to provoke a smile or signify a mood. Paste stones were arranged so that the initials of the gems they imitated

originated in England in the 17th century in the town of Woodstock, Oxfordshire. By the end of the 18th century it was highly skilful, highly expensive and the height of fashion. In much British steel jewellery, base plates were cut into specific shapes and covered with densely laid small steel studs.

The 19th century

At the outset of the 19th century, the fashion in steel jewellery spread to France, where Frichot developed a mechanical process for producing inexpensive steel pieces. In England, meanwhile, the fashion for using

The second half of the 19th century brought widescale mass-production to the fashion-conscious public. Previously, jewellery of any value had decorated only the upper echelons of society. Now, jewellery production was fast and furious, along with the manufacture of paste and other imitation stones. The 18th-century fashion for delicate and intricate white paste arrangements gave way to the more colourful, chunky and transparent paste creations of the 19th century. Cameos, pearls, gold, silver and different gemstones took turns to dominate decades. Every few years

Above (left to right):
Egyptian faience beads;
Roman gold ring; Celtic
shawl pin; Venetian glass
beads; 1830s pinchbeck
and garnet paste bracelet;
Berlin ironwork necklace;
Whitby jet earrings; gold
locket containing human hair;
pewter replica of 15th-
century pilgrim's brooch.

Overleaf (left to right):
Lalique glass brooch; Chanel
pearls; Schiaparelli earrings;
1930s bakelite pin; earrings
by Mary Quant; pearls with
paste clasp by Ken Lane;
pendant and diamanté cuff
by Christian Lacroix; 1970s
eye ring; rabbit bone and
crystal pin by Simon Costin;
heart pendant by Pam Hogg.

spelt out a modest message of love, while electro-gilded mass-market pieces were usually in the form of love trinkets such as hearts, birds or knotted branches. Jewels took on a sentimental symbolism which in many ways echoed the pagan symbolism of early jewellery. Consequently, a wealth of new materials and motifs appeared on the market. One of the most prevalent motifs was the realistic hand brooch. While in materials, human hair jewellery – an ancient tradition maintained in many African ornaments – became popular in the 1840s and 1850s in England.

Queen Victoria's love of small, dainty pieces of

The 20th century

The precious masterpieces crafted at the turn of the century by the Russian jeweller, Peter Carl Fabergé influenced the entire jewellery industry. Other early 20th-century developments included a change in emphasis for paste, which made the leap from jewellery as jewellery, to jewellery as fashion accessories. Paste has continued to be the single most important material in European jewellery production. In the 20th century, Bohemia became the main source for paste, machine-produced by Swarovski.

The languid, organic Art Nouveau style took hold in

Chanel. In the 1920s and 1930s, Chanel brought an entirely new attitude to costume jewellery, inspiring opulent, glamorous pieces that parodied the real thing, like her trademark cascades of pearls to be worn in the daytime with her understated, casual daytime jerseywear. Chanel advocated that women should be proud to wear fake jewellery – in a sense a proclamation of their new-found independence – as a sartorial gesture of defiance against the old order.

The other major arbiter of taste was Elsa Schiaparelli, who used flowers, porcelain, feathers and even ermine alongside paste stones. Her designs were bizarre and

jewellery crafted from seed pearls, semi-precious stones and an abundance of jet influenced fashions in Britain. This vogue stemmed from the way that the Queen wore jet, rather than other jewels, after the death of her consort, Prince Albert. The demand for jet (real jet is basically fossilized wood or gem-quality coal) became so great that it led to the development of imitation jets.

Another interesting 19th-century development was aluminium jewellery, which was first seen at the Paris exhibition of 1867. It was a light, welcome antidote to the ornateness of much 19th-century style.

the early 20th century, its influence spreading throughout the art and crafts of the Western world. Art Nouveau jewellery's main exponent was Charles René Lalique, who created phenomenal *objets d'art* as well as breathtaking jewellery. Art Nouveau came to an abrupt end with the advent of the First World War.

A new type of jeweller emerged in the 20th century: the fashion designer. These designers' non-precious, and occasionally precious, creations were more obviously the product of personal genius than general trends. The first in this line of artist-jeweller was Coco

bohemian, inspired by both modern movements in art – Futurism, Surrealism, Neo-classicism – and by black African art. From her vast retinue of artistic friends she commissioned memorable classics, such as Salvador Dali's telephone earrings and Jean Cocteau's eye-shaped brooch. By the late 1930s the surreal and quirky had pervaded the mainstream jewellery market.

The new technology of plastics in the 1920s and 1930s added further artistic impetus to modernist jewellery. In the 1920s a vast market for plastic Bakelite ornaments emerged. These were made in the shapes of animals and flowers – as jewellery had been since the beginning of time. Plastic jewellery was appreciated for its smooth surfaces, sculptural forms and strong colour. Of course, the proletariat wore plastic pieces, but, at the other end of the scale, Henkel and Grosse, Schiaparelli and Lalique also designed in plastic. Art Deco lent itself as a style to costume jewellery and alongside the priceless creations of Parisian jewellers like Cartier, the "new woman" looked for costume pieces with which to adorn herself. There were brooches made to look like slender Borzoi dogs, or symbols of travel – trains, boats and planes. The Bauhaus movement and the so-called

Jewellery in the 1950s was dominated by the vision of Christian Dior. His paste creations exploited radical combinations of strongly coloured glass, with scant regard for tradition. Miriam Haskell, Hobé and Hattie Carnegie were also among the more notable designers of this period.

The youth revolution of the 1960s ushered in a completely new look. A marriage of modern art and plastics technology formed the basis of Paco Rabanne's ground-breaking op-art designs. Using brightly coloured, even fluorescent, plastic discs and triangles, Rabanne made big simple geometric pieces, whose

flower power, hippies and a renewed interest in all things ethnic. The freedom in materials and approach exploited earlier in the century by the artist-jeweller spread to a wider group of craft jewellers during this period. Unusual jewellery created in home workshops by jewellers and part-time designers was available in shops and galleries all over Europe. At the end of the 1970s "punk" arrived – the final chapter in the liberation of European jewellery design. Bicycle chains, razor blades, iron crosses and safety pins joined the pantheon of personal ornaments.

Jewellery designers of the 1980s established their

Jazz Age inspired geometric chrome jewellery and the opening of Tutankhamen's tomb in 1922 exerted an Egyptian influence on design.

While fashions were still Paris-led, after the Wall Street crash of 1929, costume jewellery was a growing industry in the United States. It was inspired by Art Deco, the Hollywood film industry and the new awareness of fashion created by the burgeoning media. Although production came to a virtual halt in Europe with the outbreak of World War II, the American trade continued to develop at a rapid pace.

colour combinations and moving parts simulated the effects of op-art painting. At the same time, perhaps the first post-modern jewellery was being produced by Kenneth Jay Lane. His extraordinarily lavish concoctions of diamanté and his trademark large gilt animals plundered the historical styles of Western jewellery with a real sense of irony. He covered inexpensive plastic bangles in paste stones and snakeskin and searched out old bronzes to cast as animal heads.

In the 1970s fashion, and therefore fashion jewellery, moved from the futuristic to the nostalgic, along with

own avant-garde, creating work largely independent of trends in art and clothes, but curiously sympathetic to them. For example, Michael de Nardo creates miniature sculptures from cogs, nuts and bolts (see p.135). John Wind enjoys immense success with bracelets made from multiple linked watch faces (see p.6); Billy Boy uses plastic resin, rough stones and bold colours to create striking relief designs and Andrew Logan achieved acclaim in the 1980s with a vocabulary of broken mirror and glass, coloured stones, beading, gold and esoteric *objets trouvés* (see p.44).

The design sources of many of the jewellers whose work is illustrated in this book are as diverse as can be, but their inspirations derive from four broad categories: the materials they use; historical influences; looking at what is around them with an open mind; or a strong commitment to a concept that they want to encapsulate in their jewellery design.

Material inspirations

Time and again, jewellers will state that their main inspiration stems from the material with which they are working. Often, the jewellery will be based on their realization of how, to their mind, beautiful that material is – be it warty burr wood, like that used to such good effect by Hayley Smith (see p.52) or twisted wire, such as that used in the creations of Mary Farrell (see p.86).

unlikely and mundane of places – from supermarkets to auto-repair stations, to toy and model stores – that budding jewellery designers should keep their eyes open wherever they go and be willing to experiment with any new material that seems interesting.

The reverse process is also possible – expensive metals and precious stones can be used in a rough and raw way, denying the attributes this type of jewellery normally possesses. Tom McEwen's work (see p.115) displays this modern boldness, as does Alex Raphael's amulet and talisman necklace (see p.109), despite the exquisite workmanship.

Historical influences

History is an important influence on modern ideas and techniques in jewellery-making. You will find a huge

design sources

The jewellery then becomes an interpretation based on revealing and enhancing those aesthetic qualities and discovering how many permutations and effects they can achieve with their chosen material.

Sometimes of course, sheer happenstance takes a hand, and a chance discovery of a cache of anything from beads or broken glass to marbles, coins or shells, will provide the starting point for a new design. Frequently, the actual techniques needed to make a piece of jewellery are extremely simple, as has been shown in the many examples in this book.

Western jewellery has for so long been concerned with the aesthetics of expensive materials that the new wave of designers challenging that ethic has not yet reached its full potential. There are still so many new materials to be discovered and some in the most

quantity of books about jewellery and costume on the market, and most local libraries will stock at least a handful of the more general texts, which are usually packed with illustrations. More detailed literature will have to be researched in university libraries, art history libraries and museums.

One or several trips to a museum's jewellery department will provide you with much inspiration. Most major cities will have such a museum department (see p.140 for a selection).

Some historical eras are particularly rich in inspiration for the modern jeweller – Egyptian, Medieval, Baroque and Art Nouveau are just some of the influences that immediately spring to mind. Of course, as a budding jewellery designer, you may be inspired by the feel, look or effect of jewellery from the past. But by aiming

Right: Inspired by animals, insects and birds, this intricate collection of jewellery is made from origami. The paper is folded into shape, lacquered with a heavy-duty varnish to make it tough and water-resistant and threaded onto wire together with semi-precious stones in subtle, organic colours. The main body of each dangle earring is made from mother-of-pearl, with small, bird-shaped origami decorations. (Andrew Stoker)

to recapture or reinterpret it in different types of material, you will end up with a highly original style.

Not only can the jewellery of the past be an inspiration, so too can all of the fields of artistic endeavour. Sources quoted by jewellers range from classical architecture, paintings, costume design, fabric and rug design, medieval armour, interior design and sculpture, which, because of its three-dimensionality, is particularly important.

It is possible to borrow heavily from other artistic traditions. Roman architectural motifs, executed in miniature in modelling clay, have been used to make earrings; painted copper, echoing the appearance of old bronze sculptures, has been used to fabulous effect as a jewellery material. The shapes and motifs of prehistoric jewellery have also been an inspiration to countless jewellery designers, as have all the widely differing types of ethnic jewellery from around the non-European world. It is easy to see these influences as you turn the pages of this book.

Natural factors

All of nature – trees, flowers, plants, fruits, animals, birds, insects, rock and cloud formations, the sun, moon and stars – is a major and inexhaustible source of ideas for jewellery-making.

Whereas some costume jewellers of the late 20th century are happy to exploit artificial materials to create a contrived and sophisticated look, the dawn of a growing awareness of the value of natural products — like wood, paper and leather — means that strong references to all that is natural are now influential too (see Hayley Smith's hand-turned bangles on p.52).

Inseparable from this is the irreverence shown toward tradition by the jewellers who are represented in this book. Like the artists of the 20th century, their main motivating and inspirational force is the desire to create something new and challenging, rather than a need to slot themselves into the pattern of how things have always been done in the past.

An alternative approach is to create a recognizable, almost traditional jewellery effect through the use of unusual materials. So today much jewellery that looks quite precious may, in fact, be constructed from painted wood, paper, glass or junk materials whose origins have been cleverly disguised (draw inspiration from the work of Holli-Hallett Sullivan on p.2)

Themes and concepts

The best modern jewellery also contains a proper concept or message. Much artistic jewellery is influenced by environmental ideas – it may, for example, recycle materials in its construction, be made of natural materials, or reflect environmental concerns in any number of ways.

Other jewellery contains a strong spiritual content through the use of religious symbols and motifs or the use of materials from religious settings – for example, Julia Foster embeds Old Testament texts in copper, steel and pewter to create unique pieces of jewellery (see p.83). If you are designing your own jewellery, it is a good idea to ask yourself what are your most important beliefs and themes and then to use them as a starting point in your search for form and appropriate materials.

As well as its spiritual connotations, jewellery has often made some sort of political statement. It has been used in the past, and is still used today, as a symbol of wealth, of social standing and of marital status and there is no reason why you should not acknowledge these associations in your own work. One of the founding principles of modern designer jewellery is that beautiful things should generally be within everybody's price range – hence the use of inexpensive materials and the relatively quick execution of the pieces. Yukatek, whose work is featured throughout this book, claim that their "aim is to create jewels, which are little works of art, from non-precious materials. Each artist creates a part of the collection by hand – the unity of the collection derives from the choice of the theme and the materials used".

Another factor in jewellery design and execution is that important element of humour – much of the appeal of this type of jewellery is in its reflection of the wearer's ability to laugh at himself or herself. The wearing of conventional jewellery announces the owner's status and lifestyle: wearing jewellery that has no real monetary value or status attached to it (like Michael de Nardo's cuff bracelet made from purse clasps on p.125 or Julie Nelson's ceramic and wire creations on p.139) proclaims the wearer to be an individual.

Lightheartedness acknowledges a wide range of influences that are all rich in imagery – the cowboy hats of the American West, the New Mexican influence with its wonderful colours of pale terracotta pinks, gray-blues and silver (see Yukatek's Western-style gambling brooch pin on p.29).

Art Deco jewellers took their inspiration from machines. Now there is jewellery influenced by astrological signs, the close study of fish scales and bones and computer print-outs of body heat. With a little imagination, you will start to see the ingredients for successful jewellery-making all around you, wherever you are.

Previous pages: These clusters of cut-glass tear-drops, pyramid-shaped glass beads and papier-mâché baubles were designed in exotic colours to conjure up images of extravagant nights at fiesta time in Rio. Custom-made to complement Chris Clyne's Latin American influenced fashion collection, the faceted shapes in vibrant colours absorb and reflect the light like a child's kaleidoscope. (Olivia Dubois)

Opposite: The designer of these pieces was so fascinated by the sheer variety of shells that he saw while snorkelling in the Caribbean that it inspired him to make a "sea theme" collection of jewellery. Each natural form has been made by pouring molten pewter into a silicon rubber mould. The pieces are gold-plated and enamelled with translucent glazes to give a feel of warmer climates. (Malcolm Morris)

Although many traditional jewellery-making processes require a workshop, most of the techniques featured in this book can be carried out at the kitchen table with the bare minimum of tools. Today's "anything goes" philosophy means that you can put together delicate and sophisticated jewellery with unusual materials and the contents of a basic household toolbox.

The work area

A purpose-built jeweller's bench is not imperative for the home jeweller. In fact, many of the jewellers featured in this book started their career at the kitchen table, with no formal training. However, you should make sure that your work surface is stable and brightly lit without shadows (an adjustable lamp that clamps to the table is ideal for this purpose). A varnished wood

should be wrapped in acid-free tissue paper and stored away from light and heat. Make sure that you keep corrosive pickling acids and resins out of the reach of children in a cool, well-ventilated place.

Equipment

Much of the jewellery equipment that you need will be dictated by the medium you choose to work in. For example, metalworking processes will demand a selection of specialist tools, while paper crafts will only warrant the bare minimum of equipment – a bundle of newspaper, flour, water and a pair of sharp scissors. Your household toolbox will probably include several useful tools – for example paint brushes, a saw, a drill and fine- and coarse-grain sandpaper for wood crafts.

Perhaps the first basic item of equipment you will

equipment

table is the best surface to work on, although a plastic surface can be used instead. Although these surfaces are easy to clean, they are not heat-resistant and should therefore not be used for soldering purposes. Make sure that you keep the surface clean and dust-free at all times – especially when working with enamel or resin.

Although you don't need a jeweller's bench, you may wish to buy a jeweller's bench pin. This useful wedge-shaped tool is designed to steady and support your work and you can clamp it onto the edge of your table. A system of drawers and labelled containers (matchboxes are ideal) will keep your materials and findings tidy and dust-free. You can store ceramic and wooden beads in a glass jar, while porous semi-precious beads which are prone to fading, such as opal, rose quartz and turquoise,

need is a pair of small jewellery pliers or round-nosed pliers which you can use for shaping wire, bending head pins and opening and closing jump rings. Later, you may want to add a pair of side cutters for cutting head pins and beading wire, but a pair of scissors or wire cutters will suffice to begin with.

Many tools are versatile and can be employed in a variety of ways. For example, tweezers are ideal for picking up and holding small findings or tiny beads, but they can also be used as an alternative to round-nosed pliers for bending head pins.

Specialist tools

Eventually, you may develop a preference for working with a certain material. If you do begin to specialize in a certain technique, you will probably need a selection of specialist tools. For example, for metalwork a blow torch is probably essential as you can use it for soldering, annealing and enamelling. There are various types of torch on the market and one of the most popular is fueled by pressurized bottles of gas. These draw air through the holes situated in the burner's front nozzle and can be set to a hard flame-setting for soldering work, or to a gentler setting for heating small areas.

Many specialist tools are expensive and it is therefore not a good idea to rush out and buy them until you need them – try to make do with substitutes until you have decided which area you wish to specialize in. However, on the whole you are more likely to need paints, lacquers and papier mâché materials than metal working equipment. And you will probably prefer to

pile of beads into a pair of earrings or a decorative brooch. Choose from badge clips, chains and wires, cuff links, lockets, tie pins, jump rings, key rings and a wealth of metal stampings. There is no rule that governs what purpose each finding is designed for and the creative jeweller should investigate the findings on offer and experiment with new and original ways for using them. For a selection of findings see pages 26-27.

Jump rings, which are used to link two or more jewellery components together, are probably the most widely used jewellery finding. These circular-shaped rings are available in a range of diameters and gauges. To open a jump ring, twist the joint sideways, rather than pulling it open, to prevent the metal from weakening and snapping.

side of the clasp). Snap fasteners, which are made up of two pieces of metal that clip together, are often embellished with diamanté or pearls. They are available with between one and four links for fastening multiple strand necklaces. (See p.32 for beading equipment.)

Glue is useful for reinforcing knots and for applying sequins to fabric. The most versatile glue for jewellery purposes is a super epoxy type. This is a strong, cement-based glue that does not dry too quickly.

Brooches are among the simplest items to make and there is a wide choice of brooch backs and pins on the market to choose from. You can create interesting sculptural shapes by threading beads through the holes of a perforated disc brooch fitting with a needle and a thin wire and securing them on the reverse side. Choose

& materials

emphasize the unusual material that your pieces are crafted from – such as seaweed, pebbles and found objects – than the complicated equipment and techniques that you have employed.

Materials and findings

The vast bead emporia are a popular source for craft jewellers as they stock a wide range of beads, diamanté and metal stampings (see p.140). Flea markets and junk shops are also a good source for buying old beads, stones and glass pieces. You can even buy strings of old, broken necklaces, take them apart and use them again to make new and original creations (see p.136).

Many of the basic metal components for jewellery – findings – are mass-produced and sold by specialist retailers (see p.140). These essential pieces transform a

If you are making earrings, the first thing to decide is how the earring will be attached to the earlobe. Findings include fish hooks and kidney wires for pierced ears, or clip-on and screw-on fittings for unpierced ears. These come in a choice of base metals including hypoallergenic surgical steel. Drop earrings with moving parts are made up by threading head pins or eye pins with beads and attaching them to the earring fitting.

There are a variety of necklace clasps on the market – from heavy-duty screw types to ornate diamanté clasps and simple lightweight bolt rings (see p.26). Base your choice of clasp on the design of your necklace. A screw fastener is probably the simplest clasp and consists of two halves which screw together to form a torpedo shape (the threads are attached to the loops on either

a brooch back that suits your intended design – if you attach a narrow pin-back fitting to a heavy brooch, you may damage the fabric that you pin the brooch to.

Finish is, of course, an important factor when making jewellery and there are a wide range of finishing findings on the market. Tag-ends are probably the most common way to conceal the threads at either end of a necklace and these are available in many base metals and styles including filigree wire (see p.27). You can also attach bead caps to the fastening to hide the threads of multiple-strand necklaces.

Once you have mastered the basic techniques of working with glues and findings, you will soon feel confident enough to fashion elegant and original items of jewellery without the need for an elaborate workshop.

3-strand paste snap fastener

Bolt rings

Single-strand paste clasp

Elastic thread

Brass perforated disc brooch fitting

3-strand paste snap fastener

Aluminium brooch fitting

3-strand paste snap fastener

Bead chain

2-strand diamanté clasp

Safety bolt and chain

Screw fasteners
(torpedo clasps)

Steel chain

Tiger tail, nylon-coated steel wire

Large link aluminium chain

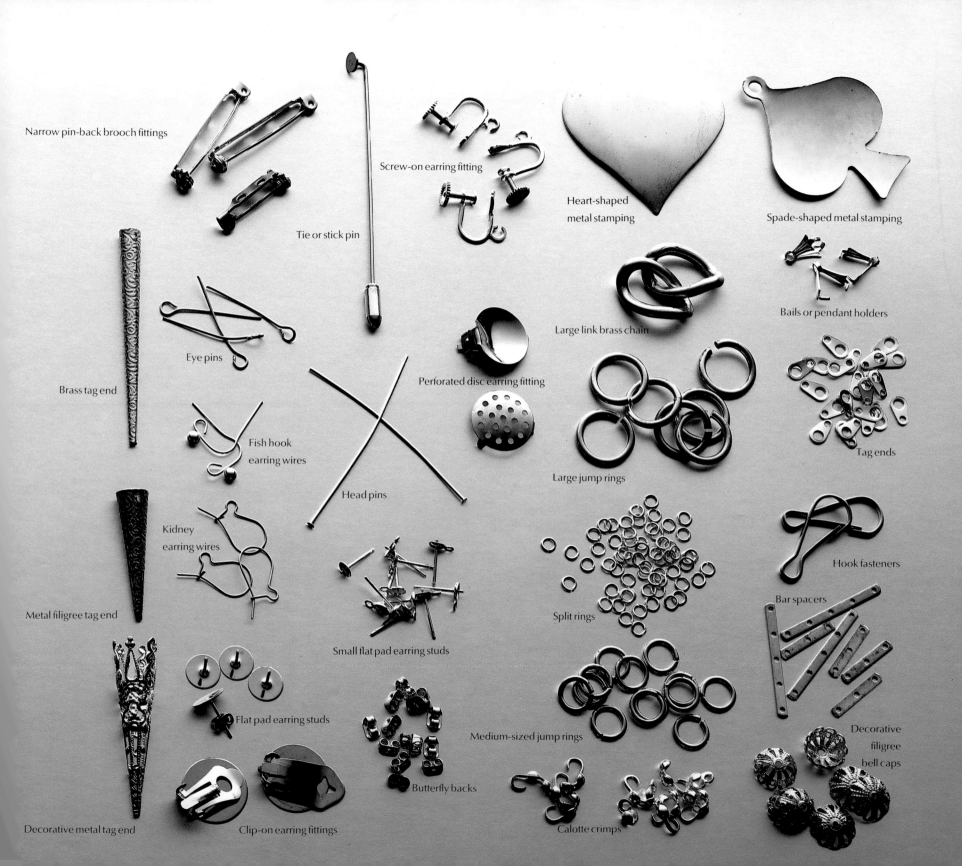

Narrow pin-back brooch fittings

Screw-on earring fitting

Heart-shaped metal stamping

Spade-shaped metal stamping

Tie or stick pin

Brass tag end

Eye pins

Large link brass chain

Bails or pendant holders

Perforated disc earring fitting

Fish hook earring wires

Tag ends

Head pins

Large jump rings

Kidney earring wires

Metal filigree tag end

Hook fasteners

Bar spacers

Small flat pad earring studs

Split rings

Decorative metal tag end

Flat pad earring studs

Medium-sized jump rings

Decorative filigree bell caps

Butterfly backs

Clip-on earring fittings

Calotte crimps

Of all the materials available to the designer jeweller, glass and ceramics are not only the least expensive, but also potentially the most sophisticated. In the form of beads, glass and ceramics can be used to make anything from a simple one-bead pendant necklace to complex woven seed-bead bangles. Glass and ceramic beads have been used for jewellery-making since the beginning of time – they have been called both "the small change of civilization" and "small handfuls of history" and have always been closely related to the technological and economical developments of civilization.

Glass

The earliest glass beads come from Western Asia and date back to the third millennium BC. However, glass beads only became widespread in Egypt by about 1400BC. The Egyptians favoured dense opaque glass, coloured to resemble turquoise and lapis lazuli, while the Phoenicians, who produced perhaps the most beautiful glass beads and pendants in the Ancient World, crafted some in the shape of tiny human heads and animals. By the 2nd or 3rd century BC, glass techniques had expanded to include folding, drawing, grinding and press-moulding. The invention of the blow-pipe during Roman times led to the first mass-production of glass beads.

Ancient glass jewellers produced a massive range of complex beads, including eye-beads, faceted beads and mosaic beads. Mosaic beads were constructed from a number of plaques – or cross-sections – which were cut from canes of patterned glass. The canes themselves were created by fusing layers of differently coloured glass together in a kiln, so that a pattern of concentric rings of colour ran through the cane's whole length. In the 14th century, Venice became the main world source for glass beads, which were traded all over the globe. Among the best-known Venetian beads are chevron and *millefiori* mosaic beads, which were constructed using remarkable manufacturing techniques: in the drawn process, a hollow globe of molten glass was attached to two metal plates with rods and two men, each holding a rod, would run in opposite directions stretching the globe into a thin, hollow cane. The resulting hollow glass tube would then be cut into thousands of beads.

The third major shift in glass jewellery-making came with the Industrial Revolution. Cut-glass beads and paste stones were developed in England, France, Bohemia and Germany which convincingly imitated cut diamonds and faceted precious stones. By the 20th century, new glass treatments, such as Tiffany's invention of iridescent fumed glass, led to the development of new beads. And moulded glass jewellery arrived with the 19th-century fashion for cameos, while Lalique created popular Art Nouveau glass pendants and brooches.

Glass beads are still produced in every corner of the world. Both Africans and native Americans integrate

glass &

Previous page left to right: Chandelier earring (Eric Beamon); star-shaped mirror brooch (Andrew Logan); charm bracelet with plastic and glass stones (Glynneth Barren); wire and marble ring (Ruth Ratner); ceramic brooch with embedded stones (Yukatek); ceramic pendant with glass beads and tassels (Karen Owens and Patrick Downing); glass marble pendant (Jane Morgan); plastic bead earrings with turquoise stones (Glynneth Barren); ceramic coiled bracelet (Karen Owens and Patrick Downing); copper lustre glass bead earrings (Annie Sherburne); eye brooch (Martin Somervail); gambling-inspired ceramic pin (Yukatek); gold-glazed ceramic drop earring (Mark Jameson); leek earring (Andrew Logan).

European beads with their own tradition of colour and jewellery design; African "*Bodom*" beads, (which literally means "to bark"), are believed to warn their owner of danger, and are fashioned from ground and often recycled glass powder. One distinctive Japanese and Korean bead is the comma-shaped "magatama". The Chinese have always produced highly complex beads, including tiny animal motifs inserted into transparent glass and decorated with wound spirals of blue glass.

Ceramics

The earliest ceramic beads date back to the 6th century BC; while the Egyptians produced glazed "faience" beads. Even though ceramic jewellery is a universal and ancient craft, until the 19th century, ceramics were the lowest in the hierarchy of jewellery materials in Europe. The Chinese made exquisite porcelain beads, decorated with enamel colours and gilded outlines, for centuries, while in Peru, the tradition is of colourful beads hand-painted with landscape and figure motifs. Clay beads, rolled between the fingers, patterned with a fingernail and left to dry in the sun are an indigenous African tradition, while in Greece, decal beads are hand-rolled and decorated with floral transfer designs.

In 19th-century Europe, porcelain became a highly prized jewellery material for cameos, beads, pendants and bracelets. Rosenthal, Meissen and the Royal Porcelain Works in Berlin produced hand-painted porcelain jewellery alongside Wedgwood in England. Italian majolica beads, decorated with religious mottos and sewn onto altar cloths, date from the 1920s.

Using synthetic clay

You can make jewellery out of many pottery materials, but most of these – earthenware, stoneware and porcelain – require firing in a kiln at temperatures well over 1,200°C (2,200°F). The fragility of ceramic jewellery limits its popularity because if you drop a ceramic earring it will probably break. However, synthetic home ceramic materials which set hard or can be baked in a domestic oven, are less breakable and therefore more viable for jewellery. Synthetic modelling clay is available from craft shops in a rainbow of colours. To use this material, start by cutting a piece of clay from the block, knead it in your hands until malleable, then, using a non-stick rolling pin, roll it out on a piece of tissue paper to smooth out the dents. Pierce any air bubbles with a pin and roll it out again into a 3mm-thin slab. Using a paper pattern as a template, cut out your required shape, embellish it with paste stones, metal powder and acrylic paint, or even try pressing graters, sieves or lace into the surface to achieve a textured finish. Fire the shape in a 225°F (130°C) oven. Leave it to cool, then apply a couple of layers of gloss or matte varnish. If you splash varnish onto the paste stones by mistake, remove it with nail varnish remover.

You can string synthetic clay shapes onto wire to make a necklace or roll a coil of clay around a cardboard tube or a glass bottle of a suitable diameter to make a bangle or armlet. If you need to create a hole for wiring, make sure that you pierce the bead with an eye pin before you bake it in the oven.

To mix colours, combine two coils of different-coloured clay and knead them well together to produce a uniform hue. For a marbled effect, roll two different-coloured coils of clay together, cut the block in two and then re-roll the two colours together. To create a multi-coloured cane (similar to seaside candy sticks), roll a piece of clay into a flat strip and coil this around a marbled piece of clay, then cut this assembly into short bead lengths.

Using beads

Glass and ceramic beads are available from a variety of sources, from flea markets and specialist bead shops to mail-order catalogues. Store loose beads in a jar to keep them clean and dust-free. Most of the equipment needed for threading beads can be found in a household tool box. Basic tools include a beading or darning needle, snipe-nosed pliers (with flat inner surfaces), round-nosed pliers, scissors and fine wire cutters. You can apply clear nail varnish or glue to knots to make them more secure, although experts decry the use of it.

The average length for an adult choker is 16in (40cm), while a standard-length necklace should be 18-in (45-cm) long and a longer-length necklace 26-in (65-cm). Necklaces which are up to 24in (60cm) in length require a fastener, but those more than 24-in (60-cm) long will fit over the head. A 32-in (80-cm) length will wrap twice around the neck. Bracelets are usually 7-in (18-cm) long, although wrist sizes vary considerably.

To establish how many beads you require for a necklace, work out how many beads there are to the inch/centimetre, then multiply that number by the total length of your necklace. For example five beads may cover an inch; multiply five by 16in and you will need 80 beads. Make sure that you allow an extra 6ins (15cms) of thread for attaching the length to the clasp.

Before you start to string the beads, lay them out on a table to establish which sizes and colourways work well together. A necklace can be as symmetrical or as random as you choose and your design may be influenced by the dictates of current fashion. Colours play an important part in design, as different-coloured beads can be cleverly mixed and integrated. You should also consider the skin and hair tone of the wearer and of course, you can design a necklace to complement a particular outfit. The following are a few examples of beading styles: a simple necklace of equal-sized beads; a symmetrical necklace with a main bead in the middle and symmetrically arranged beads on either side; a repeating necklace where the pattern repeats itself at regular intervals (this is best suited to longer necklaces); and an asymmetrical necklace.

There are a variety of threads on the market and your choice will depend on the size and weight of your beads. Make sure that you select a thread that is thin enough to pass easily through the holes in your beads, but is strong and flexible so that the necklace hangs loosely and freely. For very large, heavy beads use a fine, strong chain and for large-holed beads for pendant-style necklaces choose leather or suede thonging (stiffen the ends with adhesive tape or nail varnish for easy threading). Silk hangs beautifully and is a flexible fibre to work with, but is not very hard-wearing and

should not be wetted. Nylon monofilament (plastic fishing line) is a good choice for beads with tiny holes or where the thread needs to be rendered invisible. Nylon-coated tiger tail is the most versatile and commonly used thread as it is strong and water-resistant. Elastic thread is useful for bracelets, although it isn't suitable for heavy beads. A safety chain is an ideal precaution for securing heavy necklaces (see p.26).

To make a beaded necklace, first assemble your equipment and an assortment of beads. For a simple necklace, begin by forming a knot at one end of the thread, leaving the last 1in (2.5cm) free for holding. Place the knot in one half of the calotte and squeeze both halves of the calotte closed over it. Keeping the thread taut at all times, string the beads, making a double knot close to the final bead. Squeeze the two halves of the second calotte closed over this knot. Twist open the split loop of each calotte with pliers, hook these onto the loops at either end of the clasp and close the loops up with pliers. Finally, cut off the excess thread beyond the calottes. (If you are making a long necklace without a fastener, finish with a reef knot.)

Knotting is a more advanced technique and requires patience and perseverance (see p.36). It is by far the best way to string beads as it enables them to hang evenly. Another advantage is that if the necklace should break, you will not lose the whole length of beads.

Multi-stranded necklaces require a multiple ring clasp fastener (see p.26) and you must graduate the lengths of the strands to make them hang evenly. You will need spacer bars, which are designed to keep the threads at a good distance from each other and prevent tangling, to separate the tiers of a multi-strand necklace.

Strings of beads can also be stitched onto fabrics using an overlay or spot stitch. Another method is to sew beads onto a piece of fabric and knot the thread on the reverse. Seed beads can be strung on a thin wire and threaded onto perforated brooch and earring fittings (see p.26), offering interesting sculptural possibilities.

Above left: A wealth of semi-precious stones, ena-melled beads and decora-tive glass beads in warm mauves and lilacs have been gathered together and then tightly bound with lengths of brass wire to create this unique and richly-coloured bracelet.
(Glynneth Barren)

Right: These ornate mosaic-style pieces are created by embedding enamel shapes with a glittering assortment of tiny, brightly-coloured faceted beads, glass rocailles, bugles, semi-precious stones and sparkling diamanté stones – the result is eye-catching.
(Bradley)

how to make a **k**notted **t**hong **n**ecklace

Equipment and materials

Suede thonging 5yds
(4.5m) in length

Heavy-duty brass
three-stranded
necklace clasp

Scissors

Round-nosed pliers

Needle or wire bent to
form a needle

Fabric or leather glue
(optional)

Assorted beads to
include large, medium
and small brass beads,
10 cylindrical amber
beads, square red
beads, faceted beads,
assorted semi-precious
beads (eg. agate,
amethyst), glass and
carved beads

If you want to string a bead necklace, begin by collecting a variety of beads to work with, preferably more than you will eventually need. Spread them out on a table and move them around until you find the most pleasing arrangement. Although this necklace looks random, on closer scrutiny you will find that it has a definite bead sequence – the prominent large amber beads on each strand are interspersed with an equal number and assortment of coloured beads.

When buying beads, you will find that there is a huge selection of colours, shapes and sizes on the market. The best way to narrow down your choice is to begin by deciding on a colour theme. One approach is to look at the colours in nature to find hues that harmonize. The designer has selected rich, earthy tones, highlighted by natural red, amber and turquoise for this necklace.

If you are using a thick cord or thong, you must make sure that the beads have large enough holes to thread

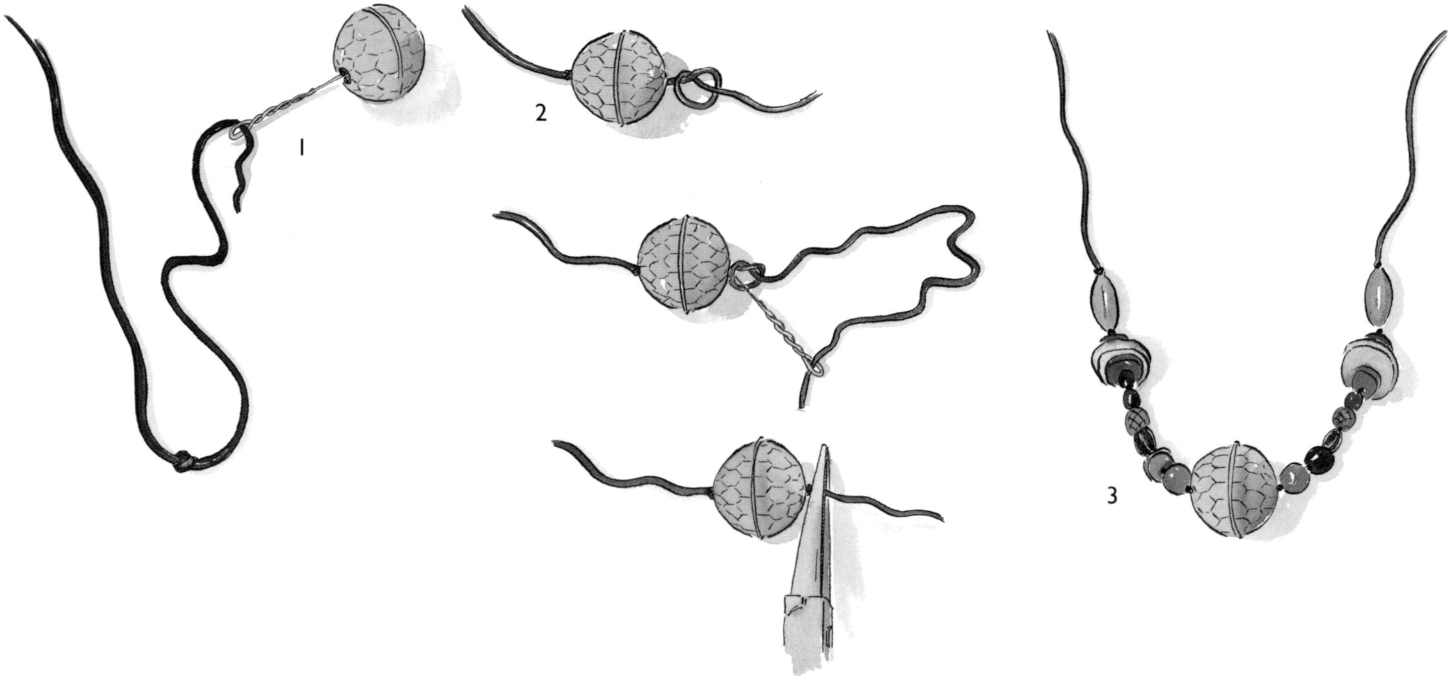

1 *For the longest strand, take a piece of thonging 5ft (1.5m) long and tie a knot a few millimetres from the central point, so that when the bead is knotted in place it lies at the central point. The finished length of the longest strand is only 30ins (75cm) long, but start with a piece of thonging that is twice that length to allow for the knots. Make your needle from a 2-in (5-cm) length of wire; bend the top third of the wire back on itself and then twist it around the top of the longer section to secure it. Thread the needle and pass it through the largest brass bead.*

2 *Press the bead firmly against the first knot in the thonging, then start to make the second knot. Form a loop on the other side of the bead and ease the new knot toward the bead with the tip of the needle. Once the knot touches the bead, pull the knot tight so that the bead stays in place. Use the pliers to make sure that the knot is pushed firmly against the bead.*

3 *Using the method detailed in step 2, string and knot the rest of the beads you have chosen for the longest strand. Knot the small beads in groups of three to four beads.*

the cord or thong through. Leather thong is available in various thicknesses and colours from haberdashery departments and craft stores. When buying thonging, you must make sure that it is strong enough to hold the weight of the beads but at the same time narrow enough to thread through even the smallest of beads. Before you start, you may need to stiffen the end of the thong with adhesive tape, clear nail varnish or glue in order to make it easier to thread.

Previous pages: A spandex bracelet assembled with Venetian, filigree and jet beads, "Magic Potion" dangle earrings and matching 5-bar bracelet and red, green and gold "carousel" bracelet with co-ordinating necklace. (Eric Beamon)

Right: You can either buy a selection of beads to make a multi-stranded necklace or break up several single-stranded necklaces that you are tired of and combine their beads to make an original new piece. (Eric Beamon)

4 *Lay the completed strand on the table and cut a shorter length of thonging to form the second, middle strand. String and knot the second strand using the same knotting method as the first. Cut a third, even shorter, length to form the innermost strand and thread and knot your beads in their chosen sequence.*

5 *To attach the clasp, first knot one end of the longest strand to the outermost link of the clasp and secure with a double knot. Next, attach one end of the middle strand to the central link of*

the clasp, then one end of the shortest strand to the innermost link, following the same method. Attach the other end of each strand to the corresponding links on the other side of the clasp. Again, secure the thonging with double knots. If the beads are very heavy, or the knots very bulky, you may need to apply a spot of glue to the knots to bond them securely. Decorate the excess thonging by knotting on small beads to make a fringe around the clasp. Trim off any excess thonging beyond the final knots on this fringe with scissors.

how to **w**ire **b**eads

Equipment and materials

Necklace

Leather thong

Large decorative glass bead

7 small glass beads of assorted shapes and colours

1 large eye pin

7 small eye pins

7 jump rings

3 large Spanish metal stampings or charms

2 brass end crimps

Round-nosed pliers

Wire cutters

Bracelet:

One spandex cuff with bead attachments

Large quantity of eye pins of various lengths

Round-nosed pliers

Assorted glass beads

You can use lengths of wired beads as pendant earrings or to decorate necklaces and bracelets. When choosing beads for a wired bracelet, bear in mind that the number of beads you require will depend on how full you want the finished bracelet to look. You can achieve different effects by varying the number and size of beads you attach to each loop on the spandex cuff. If you want a random, irregular look, attach tassels of four to five beads to every third or fourth link. If you prefer a more uniform result, link five- or six-bead tassels to all the central links and use short lengths bearing only two or three beads for the outer two link rows of the spandex cuff. For a cascading effect, thread each bead through an eye pin, cut off the excess wire and form an open loop at either end of the bead. Instead of linking these threaded beads together with jump rings as in the illustration, hook an open loop onto the open loop of an adjacent bead and close up the links with round-nosed

Necklace 1 *Thread the large eye pin through the large glass bead. Using the pliers, make a second loop at the straight end of the eye wire, making sure that the loop at the straight end is much larger than the loop at the other end. The larger loop will be used to attach the bead pendant to the leather thong (the beaded tassel will be attached to the smaller loop). Make sure that the loops fit tightly against the bead.*

2 *Thread a small eye pin through each of the small glass beads. Make a second loop at the straight end, cut off the excess wire with the wire cutters and squeeze the base of the loop together with the pliers to secure the ends. Continue in this manner until all seven beads have a secure loop at either end.*

3 *To make the beaded tassels, join two of the small wired beads together by passing an opened jump ring (see p.25) through the two loops and squeezing the join in the ring shut with the pliers. Attach a metal stamping to the end of the chain with a jump ring. Make a second chain in the same manner. For the middle tassel, join three beads together with jump rings and attach a metal stamping to the end as before.*

4 *Use the pliers to prise open the small loop at the base of the large decorative bead. Secure the three strands of beads to the large decorative bead by threading the loops at the top ends of*

pliers. As an alternative to the fluid effect of the articulated strands shown here, you can thread several beads onto one eye pin to create a rigid tassel.

There are a huge selection of beads on the market to choose from. For the co-ordinating bracelet and pendant shown on this page, Eric Beamon has chosen glass beads in warm, earthy tones and a wide range of shapes. Natural brown glass beads are interspersed with embossed brass and cool green faceted spheres.

Right: An elasticated cuff bracelet is embellished with a profusion of charms and glass beads in different shapes and sizes. Each bead is threaded onto an eye pin and these are linked collectively to form articulated strands which create a shimmering cascade effect. The pendant features a large hollow glass bead, decorated with tassels of assorted glass beads and metal stampings, suspended from a length of leather thonging.
(Eric Beamon)

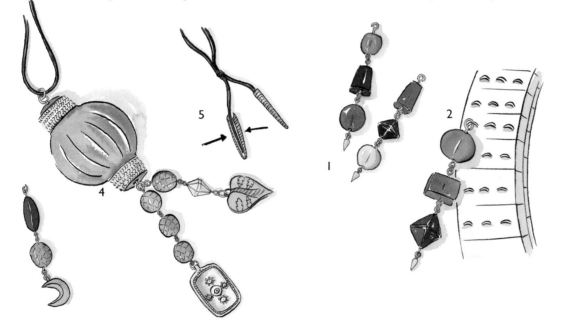

the strands through the opened loop at the base of the large bead. Use the pliers to squeeze the loop ends firmly together. Thread a jump ring onto the leather thong, open it (see p.25) and attach it to the large loop at the top end of the pendant. Make sure that the loop is secure by squeezing the join tightly shut with pliers. Knot the two ends of the thong together at the length you want, leaving about 1in (2.5cm) of thonging free beyond the knot.

5 *Neaten the ends of the thonging by fitting a brass end crimp to each end and squeezing the two halves of the crimp tightly shut with pliers.*

Bracelet 1 *Thread a small eye pin through each of the small glass beads. Make a second small loop at the straight end, cut off the excess wire and squeeze the loop together with pliers to secure the ends. To make the beaded tassel lengths, join either three or four wired beads together with jump rings (see necklace instructions, step 3).*

2 *To attach the beaded tassels to the cuff, grip the top loop in the jaws of the pliers and bend it back behind the beads to open it. Hook this loop onto the bead attachment on the cuff and pinch the ends together with pliers. Attach the rest of the tassels in the same way, working around the bracelet row by row.*

how to make a **st**ained **g**lass **p**endant

Equipment and materials

Stained glass pebbles
or marbles – 8 × 1 ½in
(3.75cm) diameter in
amber and 1 large 3in
(7.5cm) diameter in
green

Soldering iron

Solder

Copper foil, adhesive-
backed and ¼in (6mm)
wide

Reinforcing strip
(thicker copper foil)

Wood lathkin roller or
scalpel handle

Safety liquid flux

Small, soft brush

Link ring

Leather thong

Worksheet

Pickling solution

2 brass end crimps

You will need to visit a well-stocked craft shop or stained glass supplier to choose pieces of glass that blend well together in colour and texture – study the grain of the glass and decide which pebbles or marbles offer the best texture. Such a shop will also sell the other specialist equipment you require, including copper foil.

Jane Morgan's bold pieces of jewellery are based on exploiting the translucent qualities of stained glass and marbles which she buys wholesale from a specialist supplier. She started working with these elements because they are accessible, inexpensive and enable her to carry out the entire process herself without requiring complicated equipment or processes.

Although the pendant shown opposite is made from ready-cut stained glass pebbles, it is possible to cut out the pieces of coloured glass yourself. If you decide to cut out the stained glass shapes, it is advisable to practise the cutting techniques first on a piece of scrap glass. Once you have mastered the process, draw a sketch onto a piece of stained glass with a marker pen and then cut it out with a glass cutter. Always score glass on the smooth side, even if you plan to use the textured side for the finished object. When scoring glass, the blade should make a clear, rather than a grating, sound

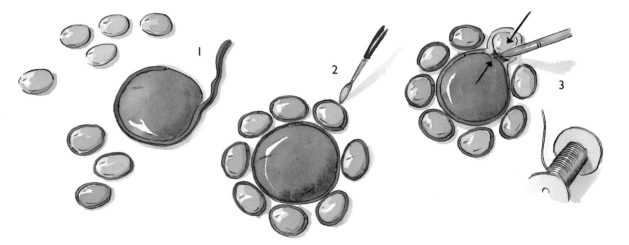

1 *Arrange the glass pebbles together to form a finished design. Choose a design that will set off the colour and transparency of your glass pebbles, but make sure that the glass pieces are clustered together so that they touch where they are to be soldered. Take the copper foil and "crimp" by moulding it firmly around the rim of each piece of glass, overlapping it slightly over each edge. Make sure that the foil is pressed firmly onto the glass using either your fingers, a wood lathkin roller or the handle of a scalpel. Next, you should use the thicker copper foil reinforcing strip to strengthen any stress points such as the*

area that the link ring will be suspended from.

2 *Position the stained glass pebbles on the worksheet ready for soldering. Switch the soldering iron on. Using a small soft-haired brush, paint the flux over the copper foil. It is important that you use flux because the solder will not flow unless the copper foil is clean. (Flux is designed to form a coating which excludes air and prevents a surface skin from forming on the metal's surface.)*

3 *Unwind some solder from the roll. Touch the tip of the solder with the tip of the soldering iron – a small amount of the*

– if you press too hard, the glass is liable to chip. To score a straight line, press the cutter wheel firmly against the glass and, starting at the furthest point, draw the cutter wheel toward you. For curves, it is easier to start at the point nearest to you and push the glass cutter away from you. After you have finished cutting out your shapes, make sure that you wash them thoroughly in hot, soapy water (this is because the solder will only adhere to a clean surface).

When working with glass and lead, it is advisable to make sure that you have had a tetanus shot in case you cut yourself.

Previous pages (left to right): A necklace of glass marbles, linked by silver jump rings; a medal brooch decorated with curls of silver wire; glass marble drop earrings; and a glass pebble necklace. Inspired by jewellery from the Romans and Celts, these pieces have an imperfect feel.
(Jane Morgan)

Right: Designed to exploit the transparent quality of stained glass, this bold pendant is fashioned from ready-made circular glass pebbles which are assembled in a flower shape and then soldered together. The completed shape is suspended from a length of leather thonging.
(Jane Morgan)

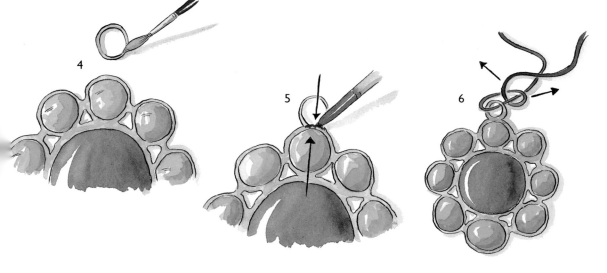

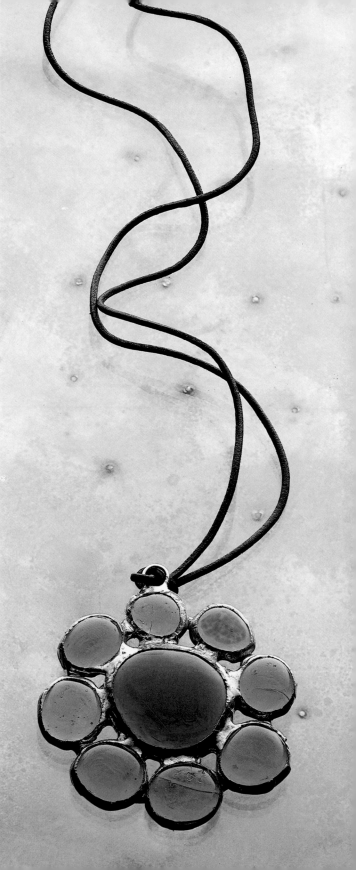

solder should adhere to the iron (if it does not, allow more time for the soldering iron to heat). Next, touch the flux-coated copper foil with the tip of the soldering iron – a little molten solder should adhere. Continue dabbing the solder on in this way until both sides of the flux-coated pebbles of glass are covered in small beads of molten solder. Push the pieces of glass firmly into place.

4 Next, use the soft-haired brush to paint a little flux over the link ring which will be used to hold the leather thong.

5 Solder the link ring to the pendant, using the method described in step 3. Once solder has cooled and set, clean your soldered pendant in a pickling solution (see p.85). Although you can use diluted sulphuric acid, this is extremely corrosive and can be dangerous if used incorrectly. Proprietary pickling solutions, usually containing alum, are safe to use and are available from jewellery suppliers.

6 Your pendant is now ready to thread onto a length of leather thong. Secure the ends of the leather thonging with a reef knot and neaten the excess thonging beyond the knot with a pair of brass end crimps (see p.26).

how to use **m**irror **g**lass

Equipment and materials

Hammer

Piece of cardboard

Resin or plastic cement
(in various colours)

Glass cutter

Pliers

Newspaper

Cocktail (swizzle)
stick

Scalpel

Mirror glass

Glass stones (assorted)

Any found objects eg.
glass eyes, broken
ceramics, shells or
sequins

Brooch clasp

Droplet pearl attached
to a jump ring

Paint and paint brush

Gold paint or enamel
paint

Sandpaper

Wire

Glue or plastic cement

When deciding on materials to use for your brooch, try to choose elements like mirror glass (make-up mirrors are best because they are thin and cheap) and stones that are relatively flat and light. Broken glass, found objects (see p.126), stones and pieces of ceramic can be transformed into a unique crazy-paving effect. You should allow yourself plenty of time to juggle with the fragments before you decide on the final layout for your piece. Don't feel restricted by the shapes you have – you can alter them with the help of the appropriate tools, for example, glass cutters, if necessary.

Gain inspiration from pictures of Indian mirrored jewellery, Greek and Roman mosaic and Aztec designs such as mirrors encrusted with coloured glass and semi-precious stones.

There are various resins and plastic cements on the

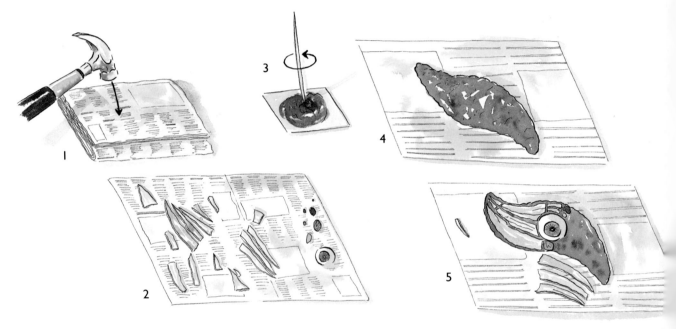

1 *Using a hammer, break the mirror glass carefully between the pieces of newspaper on a hard surface. Make sure that you hammer the mirror on the reverse side to prevent the reflective side from chipping.*
2 *Carefully play around with the resulting shards of glass until you are satisfied with the mosaic of pieces. If you want a specific shape, use a glass cutter to score across the glass and then separate the pieces using a pair of pliers. Once you are satisfied with the overall shape of your mini-jigsaw of mirror pieces, you can seek out extra decorative details – stones or any*

found objects – or just leave plain. Allow as little space as possible between the stones and the glass, as this will enhance the final effect. Set aside some small pieces of mirror or stones and use them during the construction of the brooch to fill in any gaps where the resin might show.
3 *Using a cocktail (swizzle) stick, and following the manufacturer's instructions, thoroughly mix a small amount of resin or plastic cement on a piece of cardboard.*
4 *Use some cardboard to scoop this embedding mixture onto a piece of newspaper. Then spread the mixture thinly into the*

market which are simple and versatile to use and make an ideal base for composition jewellery. Setting times will vary depending on the base material – plastic cement (chemical metal filler) takes about 3-5 minutes before it starts to harden. After the resin has dried, Martin Somervail embellishes his pieces by coating any undecorated areas of resin with a couple of layers of black enamel or gold paint.

Previous pages: These colourful and imaginative pieces are made using reflective mirror glass which is embedded in resin and embellished with jewels, glitter and found objects.
(Andrew Logan)

Right: Fashioned from shards of mirror glass which are set in resin, these brooches are also decorated with found objects – the Victorian glass eye was found at a flea market.
(Martin Somervail)

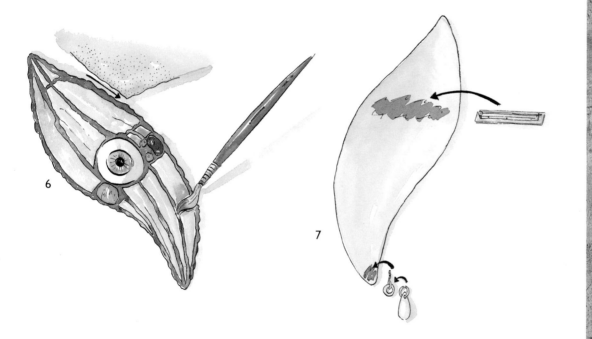

same shape as your assembly of glass shards.

5 *Working quickly but carefully, arrange the mosaic pieces in the embedding mixture. You will have three to five minutes to rearrange the pieces before the mixture starts to set. Check that all the edges are anchored by the plastic. Once the main brooch has hardened, if there are any sharp edges left uncovered simply mix up some more embedding mixture and apply a thin layer over these edges.*

6 *After about 10 to 20 minutes, the mixture should be completely set. Tidy up any rough edges by scraping them with*

a scalpel and smoothing the sides with sandpaper. Using a small paint brush, apply your chosen colour to the exposed resin between the sections of mosaic.

7 *Turn the brooch over and attach the brooch clasp using resin, plastic cement or glue. If you don't want to leave the back plain, you can paint it with enamel or gold paint. To attach the small droplet pearl, thread it onto a jump ring. Make a wire loop with a tail and link it to the pearl with a jump ring. Attach this wire loop to the base of the brooch with resin, plastic cement or glue.*

Perhaps the best-known item of wooden jewellery, whether painted, hand-carved or simply cut and varnished, is the crucifix. Since wood has not been used extensively for jewellery-making, its history is not as easy to chronicle as that of jewellery made from other materials. It appears, however, that wood has been used both for mass-market pieces and for items worn by the nobility. The Victoria and Albert Museum in London, England (see p.140) has on display an exquisite 14th-century chain belt carved from a single piece of wood and decorated with the arms of Brittany. It is highly likely that tiny wooden reliefs were worn as pendants in the principal wood-carving regions of the Middle Ages and early modern period, such as Southern Germany.

expanded dramatically in the 1970s following a general interest in natural materials at that time. A number of jewellery designers produced work in wood, for example Alexandra Anne Dick and Matthew Tomalin, while Angela Cummings designed wooden pieces for Tiffany and Co. in New York.

Wooden beads

Today, beads are made in an immense variety of woods and styles all over the world. The colour and grain of different woods provides their interest and individuality; some woods are fragrant too. Beech, boxwood, ebony, pine and sandalwood are commonly used for making beads. Bamboo, being hollow, is one of the most popular materials, while stem wood from bamboo

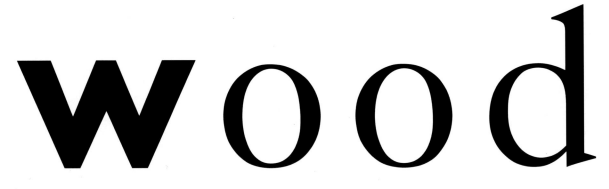

wood

And it is also thought that prehistoric man carved beads from wood.

African tribes are recognized for their wooden pendants and beads, while Japan and China both have traditions for ornate sculptural beads and since the 17th century, Japanese craftsmen have fashioned hair combs and pins from wood. These were often hand-painted with patterns, figures or landscapes in toothcomb designs which always beautifully integrated the curved shape of the comb.

Wooden jewellery occasionally came into fashion in 19th- and 20th-century Europe. In the 1930s, wooden bracelets made up of prisms of inlaid hardwood strung on elastic were worn. Wooden jewellery manufacture

or palm trees is soft enough to be moulded into almost any shape. Temperate hardwoods such as yew, walnut, oak and holly are also used for bead-making, but tropical hardwoods like rosewood, Brazilian mahogany and tulip-wood are becoming less popular because of growing fears about deforestation.

Other parts of the tree can be used for bead-making too: the people of the Philippines are known for their banana leaf beads, which they produce by gluing and lacquering banana leaves onto a basic wooden shape. They also produce layered beads by sandwiching different varieties of wood together. Cork, from the outer bark of the cork oak tree, can occasionally be found crafted into beads.

Wooden beads can be carved, hand-painted, lacquered, varnished or stained to imitate ebony, while some Indian beads are inlaid with mother of pearl or twisted brass wire. Carved wooden beads, crafted with a revolving tool that cuts circular grooves around the circumference of the bead, are highly attractive. The best source for buying wooden beads is from a specialist bead shop (see p.140).

Sam Ubhi (see p.49), who trained as a textile designer, makes jewellery and home accessories such as candlesticks and lamps. Her jewellery is all hand-made and she particularly likes working with wood because it has such a smooth, natural feel which works well with the rich silks that she loves to use. "I am Indian which means that I love bright colours and texture." Sam dyes her wooden beads with commercial fabric dye, which she buys from a hardware store.

Hand-painting wood
Decorated wooden shapes make very attractive earrings and brooches, even necklaces. The tools you will need for this sort of jewellery are simple – a small fret saw or piercing saw, a drill, a vice, sandpaper in various grades or an electric sanding machine for speed, assorted enamel or gouache paints, varnish and a selection of paint brushes. The most suitable wood for jewellery-making is plywood since it is lightweight and can be obtained in thin sheets which can be easily cut into your required silhouette. Also, differently shaped pieces can easily be glued together with an appropriate wood glue. Annie Sherburne works in this medium to brilliant effect (see p.57 for instructions).

Annie experiments with different combinations of paints to decorate her pieces. For example, one of her methods is to apply a water-based paint over a base coat of oil paint which she then varnishes to preserve the design. For a "cracked", textured surface, she uses an oil paint base coat with a top coat of cellulose paint. Another variation is to spray auto paint (which is very unecological) over an oil-based base coat – this gives a bubbly, crinkled finish. After the paint has dried, Annie sands and varnishes the surface before decorating it with gold paint.

Annie Sherburne gains her inspiration from hand-painted Indian papier-mâché jewellery. She has also been influenced by the jewellery of the African Massai tribe, as were the musician Boy George and the fashion designers Bodymap in the early 1980s. A third influence was the work of the Bloomsbury Group, especially at their Omega Workshop, early in the 20th century. Their idea of craftsmanship, whereby a commune of artists made real objects for real people's homes, took William Morris' and John Ruskin's "Arts and Crafts" idea a stage further.

Annie Sherburne first started making jewellery on her return from India and based her designs on her impressions of the country, with combinations of gold cord, painted wooden beads and diamanté. "It was meant to represent a joyous approach to life". She uses accessible materials for her highly decorative pieces. "For me, jewellery is a very complex thing with an aesthetic, historical and contemporary aspect."

In 1983, the British fashion designer Jean Muir discovered Annie Sherburne at an exhibition in London entitled "Jewellery Redefined" where the work of well-known and up-and-coming jewellery designers was on display. It was at this influential British exhibition that a major shift in jewellers' materials and the prevailing attitude to jewellery became apparent. Jean Muir commissioned Annie to hand-paint wooden buttons for her studio collection. She soon began to handpaint wooden jewellery for Jean Muir and produced her own collections at the same time.

Woodcarving
Paint is not the only decorative possibility for wooden jewellery – woodcarving is worth considering too. The best wood to use for this is a hardwood like beech or sycamore which, although it is more difficult to carve than softwood, will survive more wear and tear. Small

Previous page left to right: Sycamore cuff with toggles (Naomi James); turquoise stained and laminated bangle (Hayley Smith); inlaid segment bracelet (Yukatek); stained wooden heart brooch (Cynthia Rybakoff); hand-painted wooden beads (Annie Sherburne); metal and cork cuff (Yukatek); bleached

wood beads (Sam Ubhi); sycamore and silver brooch (Carlo Giovanni Verda); inlaid sycamore bangle and ring (Naomi James); cocobolo and tulip-wood beads (Heart of the Woods).

Above: Hand-painted wooden drop earrings. (Yukatek).

tools are essential for carving pendants and brooches – flat-edged chisels, gouges, rifflers (small file-like abrasive metal tools with serrated surfaces), sandpaper in various grades and steel wool.

Make sure that you make a hole for a pendant cord before you start carving the wood bead and seal the finished surface with a wax polish or varnish to enhance its colour and grain.

Carlo Giovanni Verda (see p.48) crafts his jewellery from silver, granite and hand-carved sycamore wood. He takes his inspiration from Stone Age tools and weapons, binding his brooches with silver to imitate the techniques employed by prehistoric man to bind a handle to a tool or knife. He recommends that you use small chisels and wood rasps for carving wood and that you work with wet wood, steamed first in the oven to make it flexible. He buys sycamore, which is very smooth and takes stain well, from a local wood merchant, cuts it out with a jeweller's saw, stains it with commercial stain (available from hardware stores) and files it smooth. If he is making a bead, he punctures it with a craft knife or fine drill and threads the silver wire through the wood.

Wood-turning

A specialist craft, wood-turning involves the use of a lathe. Hayley Smith, who has been making wood-turned bangles for two years, warns that wood-turning can be dangerous because you have to know how to hold the tool to the spinning wood. Make sure that you wear a helmet and face shield while working with a lathe and avoid inhaling any sawdust, especially from tropical wood, as it is unhealthy.

Hayley buys a whole tree at a time – she cuts it into moveable pieces with a chain saw and takes it home in a trailer. At home, she cuts the wood into blanks – blocks of wood from which she can cut bangles. The blank is screwed onto the lathe and turned. She cuts the wrist opening out with a parting tool. Each bangle takes about two hours to make.

For Hayley, selecting wood is the most important process, as it is the grain of the wood that she likes to emphasize. She uses special burr wood from oak, elm or yew. (Burrs are the knotty wart-like protrusions from trees.) "My bangles have a very natural rough-hewn quality – there are cavities in them where the bark would have been, since the wood comes from near the surface of the tree. Burr wood is cut wet and, instead of splitting like straight-grained wood does, it shrinks because its grain is knitted together. You can achieve an incredible texture, depending on whether you cut it across its length or cross-section". After cutting the bangle, she may microwave the piece for a minute to dry out the wood and improve its texture.

Hayley has been influenced by other wood-workers, especially Jim Partridge. She has also gained inspiration during her frequent visits to the Pitt Rivers Museum in Oxford, England, (see p.140) which has a large collection of ethnic jewellery on display, including a selection of pieces made from natural materials.

Wood finishes

There are endless techniques for finishing wood and many of the finishes outlined in furniture restoration books and woodwork manuals can be applied just as readily to items of wooden jewellery.

Among the techniques employed by Hayley Smith are scorching turned bangles with a blow torch to highlight the grain of the wood or completely singeing them to achieve a warm, black colour. Another technique Hayley has developed is to colour bangles with a solution of vinegar and rusted steel wool, which can be used to blacken elm and oak wood. To make this dye solution, put a lump of steel wool in malt vinegar and leave it to rust and dissolve for about a month before applying it to the surface of the bead with a soft cloth. Another method for finishing wood is to put freshly turned oak into a tank of fuming ammonia – the oak will acquire an antique look, as if it has been darkened with time. Hayley uses liming wax to whiten

wood, which gives it the appearance of having been washed up on the beach. And sandblasting can be used to etch out the softer fibres, bleaching and texturing the wood's surface.

Once she has finished work on her chosen surface, Hayley oils her bangles with Danish oil to protect them and improve their texture. This is fast-drying and soaks readily into the wood. She applies two coats and rubs each one in well, waiting for the first to dry properly before applying the second coat. Then she polishes her bangles with beeswax.

If you don't want to turn wood, you can experiment with these finishing techniques on pieces of driftwood or offcuts of carved wood, although different woods will react in different ways to each finish.

Wood is an underrated material for jewellery. Not only is it lightweight, warm, strong and inexpensive, but it also has infinite variations of grain and texture that grow more interesting and marked as the piece ages and wears.

Previous page: These bangles are all crafted from burr wood which has been selected for its unique appearance. The wood, which is sourced from oak, elm or yew trees, is hand-turned on a lathe and finished in a variety of ways. Some bangles are microwaved to improve their texture, while others are scorched or polished to highlight their grain; some are sandblasted to bleach the wood, while others are decorated with string or brass nails. (Hayley Smith)

Opposite: Three bold, hand-painted wooden brooch designs. Each piece has been decorated with several coats of enamel or gouache paint and then highlighted with gold paint.
The painted brooches have been embellished with faceted droplets and cabochon stones in different sizes and colours to add interest and sparkle to the designs. Faceted stones are particularly striking because they glisten when they reflect the light. (Annie Sherburne)

how to make **w**ooden **e**arrings

Equipment and materials

Workbench

Plywood

Fine-grade sandpaper

Coarse-grade
sandpaper

Fretsaw

Sanding machine
(optional for speed)

Vice

Hand-drill, with very
fine drill bit

Cardboard

Pencil

Compass

Ruler

Scissors

Enamel or gouache
paint

Assorted glass stones

2 earring findings

Clear polyurethane
varnish

PVA or white glue

Crystal drop beads

18 jump rings

Fine paint brushes

Decide on the shape and design you would like to make and then draw it to scale, indicating the surface painting and the applied stone decoration. Annie Sherburne uses gouache paints for her pieces, which are available in a huge range of rich, bright colours. She takes her inspiration from hand-painted Indian and Kashmiri boxes and miniature paintings, from ancient South American symbols, from the decorative products of the Omega workshops and from 20th-century abstract painting techniques.

Although there are a myriad of shapes you can combine to make your earring, you should make sure that you pay attention to the proportion between the two elements. The pair of earrings shown opposite are embellished with faceted drop stones, cabochon-style stones and sequins – these are particularly effective

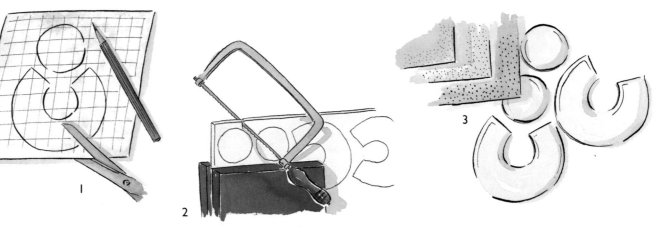

1 *To make a template shape, take a piece of thin cardboard and accurately draw two separate shapes – in this instance a circular disc measuring 1in (2.5cm) in diameter and a crescent shape resembling a squashed horseshoe, which will become the suspended section. When you are satisfied with the flat design silhouette, simply cut out both cardboard pieces with scissors.*

2 *Place the crescent and circle shapes flat onto the plywood and draw around them with a pencil twice to create a pair. Leave as little space as possible between the shapes as this makes the plywood easier to cut out once in the vice. Clamp the plywood in a vice secured to a workbench. Take the fretsaw and cut out the shapes. (Work cautiously as fretsaws have very thin blades which are easily fractured if too much tension is applied.)*

3 *Once you have cut out and released the shapes from the rest of the plywood, tidy up the edges. Sand and then bevel or chamfer the edges of both shapes to give a professional finish.*

Use a hand-held sanding machine or simply sand manually to achieve a satisfactory finish. Once your pieces are smoothly bevelled, remove all loose sawdust particles.

4 *Apply the base coat of paint to the reverse sides of the wood shapes and leave them to dry. Once dry, turn them all over and paint the fronts in the same way. If necessary, repeat the procedure for a denser colour. Apply the paint decoration on top of the dry base coat. After you have finished your painted design, leave the pieces to dry before applying the varnish. Seal the painted shapes with a layer of clear polyurethane varnish and leave them to dry in a dust-free place. Once fully dry, lay the shapes on a flat surface.*

5 *Place the crescent shape underneath the wide disc, making sure that the disc shape is exactly ½in (1.25cm) above the crescent's highest corner points and that the pieces are absolutely symmetrical. You can now estimate and mark the position of*

because of their reflective quality. When painting your wooden pieces, endeavour to co-ordinate your design details by simultaneously creating spaces for mounting the glass stones and beads. For example, a row of repeated painted loops in a curve can have a stone applied to the middle of each loop, enhancing the pattern and lending a three-dimensional effect to your flat design.

Right: Three striking examples of decorated plywood earrings. Each earring is hand-painted in a unique and intricate pattern with brightly coloured enamel or gouache paint. They are embellished with faceted glass stones, seed beads and other small found objects. Plywood is obtainable in thin sheets and its light-weight nature makes it an ideal choice of material for large-scale pieces. (Annie Sherburne)

the drill holes that will be linked by jump rings to connect both shapes (one is suspended from the other). Mark all holes with a sharp implement (eg. the point of your compass); there are eight holes to mark in total. The top circular disc must be marked at three points; the first point is the central point of the suspended crescent. Next, mark left and right of this point on the circle, judging these points in relation to the highest corner edges of the lower crescent shape. Mark these two points on the crescent shape too. Finally, mark three holes on the bottom rim of the crescent. Place the first one symmetrically and then mark one either side of this, with ¾in (2cm) intervals between holes.

Take a hand-drill with an extremely fine bit and drill out holes in all marked positions. Take care not to drill too close to the edge as this may cause the wood to split and fracture.

Link the two painted shapes together with jump rings. Bend the rings open with your fingers (see p.25) to create six sets of three linked jump rings. Attach three of these jump ring chains to the three holes at the bottom edge of the crescent by bending open the top link of each chain and threading it through the drilled hole. Finish the other end of each chain by attaching a droplet crystal stone at the bottom. Attach the three remaining sets of links to the holes in the circular disc top section. Thread a fourth crystal drop onto the end of the central dangle and link these directly to the left and right corner holes of the horseshoe shape.

Embellish your pattern with glass stones. To attach a flat-backed stone simply apply a small blob of glue to the painted surface. Some stones have a bevelled back; in order to mount this type of stone you must cut a small pointed dip out of the flat wood – either use a scalpel or slightly drill the surface. Sit the stone comfortably in the dip and glue it in place. Once you have glued all the stones in place and the glue has dried, turn each earring over and glue a finding to the back of the top circle.

Paper is inexpensive, versatile, easily accessible and, above all, lightweight, which is why it is fast becoming such a popular medium for contemporary jewellery designers to work with. Today, there is renewed interest in paper-making generally. In the past, the paper-making process was a means of recycling a material whose time-consuming and limited production made it expensive. Today, with recycling once again at the forefront of our minds (only this time with the emphasis on the deforestation of the rainforests), paper craft is very much in vogue. Paper is not only an environmentally friendly craft material, it is also a money-saver because most of the materials needed for making paper jewellery can be found in the home.

also be embedded with stones, found objects and beads. With a little imagination and skill, it can be used in all sorts of ways to produce jewellery of any shape or size, for relatively little cost.

Papier mâché

Literally translated as "chewed paper", or arguably as "mashed paper", papier mâché is the most familiar of all paper art forms. Invented in China in the 2nd century AD, the art of pulping and moulding paper caught on in the West during the 18th century. The French made it a commercially viable art form and the trend took off in England, where production was at its greatest. Soon even the Russians began to emulate English designs. In 1883, papier mâché proved its worth as a jewellery

Previous pages left to right: Dangle earrings (Nieuwe Nomaden); "pebble" necklace (Jeannell Kolkman); marbled paper ring (Alexa Wilding); laminated paper brooch (Hammine Tappenden); chunky bangle (Lynette Garland); gilded brooch (Gill Clement); gilded cuff bracelet (Holli Hallett-Sullivan); Julius Caesar brooch (Marion Elliot); witty knife and fork brooches (Julie Arkell);

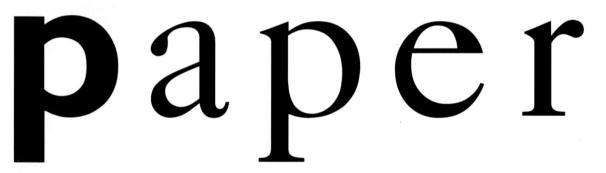

paper

Papier mâché is the most recognized paper craft technique, but for jewellery paper can be used in other ways. Lesser known, but just as effective, techniques include laminating and origami. The lightweight and malleable properties of paper suit the current European trend for jewellery that works with the body as a "body sculpture", rather than just as ornamentation. Julia Manheim's papier mâché bangle on p.64, which stretches from wrist to arm, exemplifies contemporary "body sculpture".

Jewellers who work with paper strongly advocate its chameleon-like qualities, for a piece of paper can be transformed to look like many different elements. Paper can be made to imitate resin, wood, plastic, marble or even highly polished brass (see p.2). It can

material, when the first-ever watch to be constructed from paper was created in Germany.

During the 19th century, papier mâché was used widely in Britain and the United States to make a variety of common household objects – many homes still possess one of the ubiquitous flower-decorated trays. By the 1920s, a surplus of papier mâché products on the British market and the popularity of the new "electro-plated" goods marked the end of the papier mâché boom. But today, after a long period out of favour, papier mâché is once again popular.

The traditional methods upheld by rural communities in Kashmir, Mexico and Japan are still employed by contemporary Western designers, but adaptions have been introduced for faster and easier production.

large teeth brooch (Julia Manheim); laminated paper earrings (Kate Smith); marbled paper and wooden bead necklace (Alexa Wilding).

Opposite: These opulent cuffs and brooches are made from thick, hand-made Indian paper. This is scored and then painted by hand in rich shades and decorated with faceted stones.
(Gill Clement)

There are two main papier mâché techniques — pulping and layering. The first involves the mashing of paper with water, which is then put into a mould or made into a solid shape; the second involves roughly tearing strips of paper and wrapping them around a mould, then pasting and drying each layer. The pulping method entails more preparation than the layering technique, but needs drying only once. Layering is the most widespread method and is based on the gradual accumulation of paper; the finished product is more fragile than a pulped piece.

Lynette Garland, whose jewellery is featured overleaf, uses the pulped method. Although you can use any kind of paper for this process, Lynette uses tissue paper soaked overnight and then heated for 20 minutes on a stove. She prefers to mix the paper, PVC or white glue and chalk or whiting in a food blender, but you can combine the ingredients in an ordinary mixing bowl. (Wallpaper paste or flour blended with water can be used instead of a PVC or white glue.) The substance is then poured into a greased mould (usually made from plaster of Paris or clay) and left to dry for two days. Once it is hardened and completely dry, the papier mâché shape is removed from the mould and smoothed with a file to remove any rough edges.

Papier mâché is an art which redefines the term artist-jeweller. Many of the designers contributing to this section see themselves as mini-sculptors and have gone on to work in sculpture. This is true of Julia Manheim, whose papier mâché pieces are featured on p.64. Julia constructs her jewellery by building layers of papier mâché around a wire frame, but for her sculptures, she uses crumpled newspaper and metal, inserting the papier mâché substance inside the metal wire frame.

It is easy to criticize the "unwearability" of some jewellery, but Alexa Wilding has begun working on totally "wearable" sculptures, such as her marbled bead necklace (see p.58). The texture and ingrained pattern of her pieces depend upon the unique construction of her papier mâché technique, which she keeps largely a secret. What Alexa will reveal is that she sculpts sturdy pieces of papier mâché criss-cross fashion, without the use of a mould, which she then leaves to dry over a period of two months.

Because the layering technique is such a lengthy process, individuals have failed to agree on how much time should be allowed for pieces to dry. Although it is recommended that each layer of papier mâché should be left to dry before a new one is applied, some designers prefer to dry two or three layers at one time, while others prefer to wrap and dry all the layers together. The drying process can be speeded up by putting the pieces in a low-heat oven or on a radiator.

Julie Arkell also uses the layering technique for her jewellery. Her work is identifiable by its mosaic finish, which is created by applying found objects such as glass, stones and broken china to a whitewashed surface. For this purpose, like the designers featured in the Found Media section (see p.124), Julie is also inspired by urban "jewels" such as broken bottles, pieces of broken auto headlight and anything which sparkles. She has even made jewellery containing fragments from an orange indicator light, giving new meaning to papier mâché as an ecologically sound medium. Like many designers, Julie builds her work around a template, which she makes from scraperboard or cardboard strengthened with linseed oil. Moulds are equally usable and long balloons form a good basis for bangles; while Holli Hallett-Sullivan supports her jewellery on a frame made of filling compound (spackle), cardboard tubes or coathanger wire — these elements give her jewellery deliberately uneven edges.

As well as the paper itself, surface decoration can also be applied using a layering technique. Julia Manheim uses layers of colour to "highlight the different layers" of paper. And Dutch designer, Jeannell Kolkman, achieves an irregular pattern by printing layers of different colours onto her outermost sheet of paper,

Above: Despite the fact that this jagged-looking golden bangle looks like it has been structured from metal, it is actually made from papier mâché which has been built around a metal coathanger armature. It is then gilded with gold leaf and polished.
(Holli Hallett-Sullivan)

allowing each colour to dry for 20 minutes. She then applies the resulting unique paper to papier mâché pieces such as brooches, earrings and hair ornaments.

Laminating

Another common process is laminating: this method is especially popular among Dutch jewellers. There are a variety of coated papers suitable for laminating on the market; these have been specifically designed for cutting and folding (see p.140 for suppliers).

Hammine Tappenden and Kate Smith both produce laminated paper jewellery. While Kate uses pre-coloured paper which she decorates after lamination, Hammine paints her own paper before she begins the laminating process or alternatively begins with a collage made from silver foil or candy wrappers. Laminating machines can be found in most print stores (see p.140 for a list of addresses). Lamination is a method of heatsealing the paper to give it a robust and durable plastic texture with a flat, shiny surface. Once the sheets have been laminated, shapes are cut out with a leather punch or a darning needle and worked into jewellery. Sequins or beads can be applied with a strong adhesive after lamination. The beauty of lamination, as described by Kate Smith who works in different forms of papier mâché, is that "it is less time-consuming than other techniques and allows for mass-production".

Origami

The Japanese art of paper folding is another excellent way of using pre-coloured or pre-treated paper to make jewellery. Origami is a traditional art form which has been handed down to Japanese children for over 400 years. Unlike many traditions, the art of origami is still widely practised today in its country of origin – Japanese department stores are constantly exhibiting new pieces. Origami is also practised in the West, in particular in the United States, where artists have created complex three-dimensional shapes. Origami serves both ornamental and ritualistic functions in Japan, where it is used for making ceremonial ornaments and tools.

According to Andrew Stoker, whose paper birds and insects are featured on p.19, the real skill of origami for jewellery-making purposes, especially earrings, is to create an origami piece that hangs evenly.

Andrew prefers to hand-marble paper himself, rather than using pre-treated varieties. This old Syrian art involves literally floating coloured inks on water. While the process can be controlled to a certain extent, every pattern will be unique. Once dry, the paper is folded and the shapes are lacquered with a heavy-duty varnish to make them tough and water-resistant.

The importance of finishing and lacquering paper jewellery cannot be underestimated. The glossy effect on papier mâché pieces is achieved by applying coats of lacquer, often in conjunction with gilding. There are several methods for gilding papier mâché. For instance, Lynette Garland uses gold size for securing real gold leaf. She then coats the gilded article with a protective layer of transparent, waterproof paint. While gold leaf is very popular with jewellery designers, beginners often prefer less expensive Dutch metal (available in gold, silver and copper colours). Holli Hallett-Sullivan, another gilding veteran, uses button polish, a brownish, sticky substance, both to secure small pieces of gold leaf and to glaze jewellery. She often employs a dozen or more coats to achieve a satisfactory shade of gold. Alexa Wilding's shiny metallic effects are achieved by using silver or gold paper treated with up to 26 coats of varnish.

There are no strict rules to follow when working with paper. The great charm of much paper jewellery, especially papier mâché, is its rough and random texture and its total lack of severe structural form. Wrapping paper, gold and silver foil, computer paper and candy wrappers can all be used to create interesting pieces which can then be decorated with anything from fabric remnants and beads to artificial flowers. Take an imaginative look at all of the wastepaper products in your home before throwing them away – you will be surprised by how many of them you can turn into jewellery.

Above: Influenced by classical themes, this bangle is also constructed from papier mâché. The tissue paper is first soaked overnight and then poured into a greased mould where it is left to set. Once it is dry, it is smoothed with sand paper and painted.
(Lynette Garland)

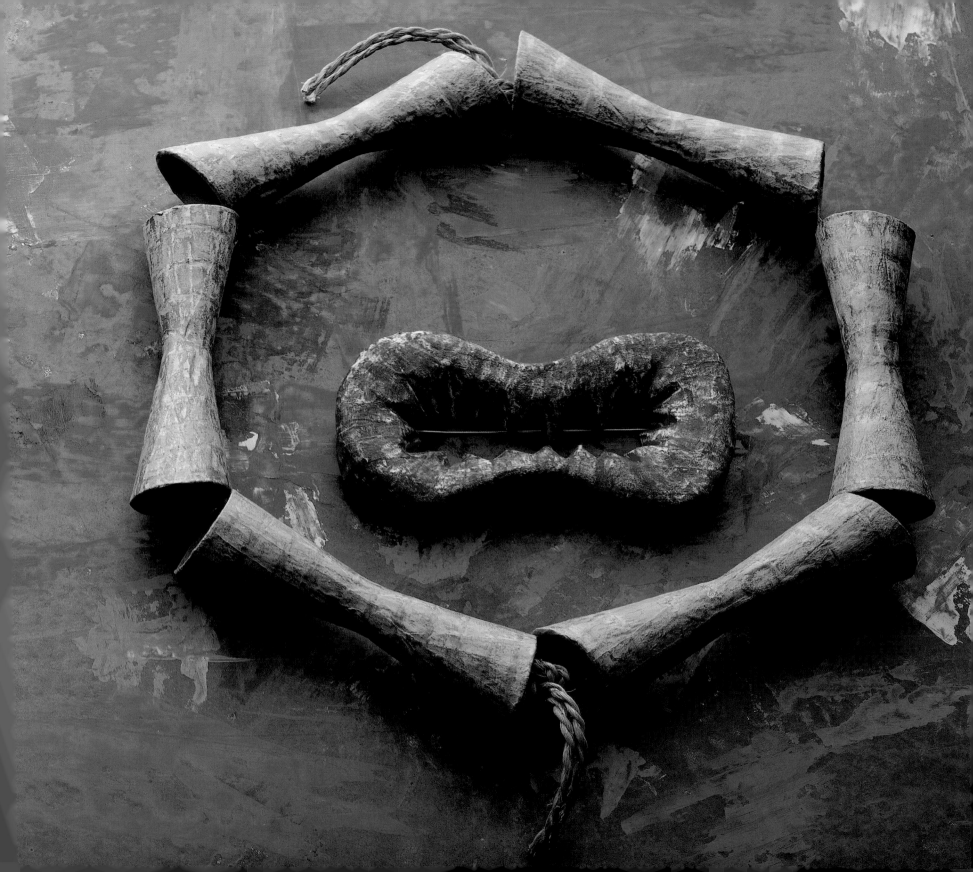

how to make **p**apier **m**âché earrings

Equipment and materials

Good quantity of
newspaper

Wallpaper paste

PVA or white glue to
seal

Cardboard

6 jump rings

Drop stones

Earring findings

Enamel or gouache
paint

Variety of fine paint
brushes

Scalpel

Compass

Pliers

Pencil

Epoxy glue

Scissors

Dish or container

Papier mâché is inexpensive and quite simple to make. It involves saturating paper until it forms a pulp, then mixing in wallpaper paste or flour and water.

Alternatively, papier mâché items can be structured from strips of paper layered with wallpaper paste. And you can use cardboard, wire or other light materials as a skeleton or armature upon which to fashion your chosen jewellery design.

Marion Elliot has been working in layering since 1988. Her personal papier mâché method is to use heavy cardboard sandwiched with paper, which she then cuts out in her chosen shape and covers with several strips of glued newspaper to create a narrow three-dimensional form.

Experiment with a variety of papers including newspaper, sugar paper, cartons, cardboard and tissue paper. Newspaper will produce a coarse pulp, while tissue paper will produce a fine-textured one.

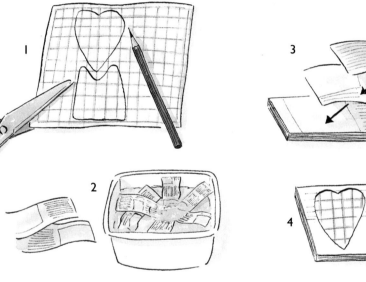

1 *Compose your design, sketching it out on paper. In this example, the top section is a heart shape and from this a larger, more irregular, shape is suspended. They are joined centrally by a jump ring. The two accompanying shapes can take any form you like – experiment on paper until you are satisfied with your design. The finished design should have an irregular spontaneous feel; don't try to create perfect symmetry. Draw your final design onto cardboard and cut out the two cardboard shapes. These will serve as the basic structure on which to bind the strips of papier mâché. Alternatively, for a more three-dimensional effect, make an inner armature of sandwiched newspaper.*
2 *Cut a small section of a fully closed newspaper with sharp*

scissors; this will give you a large quantity of small pieces quickly. Next, crush these pieces into a dish or container filled with a mixture of wallpaper paste and water.
3 *Once they have absorbed a sufficient amount of paste, but are not yet saturated, remove them and, with your fingers, construct a layered sandwich of the small sheets. Leave this sandwich to dry.*
4 *Using your two cardboard templates and a pencil, draw around each shape twice (to make a pair of earrings) onto the dried newspaper sandwich. Cut out the shapes carefully using a scalpel or a sharp craft knife.*
5 *Take thin strips of newspaper and brush each one with more wallpaper paste. Bind each shape neatly with the strips*

Once dry, you can either smooth the finished surface with sandpaper, carve it to create a pattern or simply decorate it with paint and stones. You can use any type of paint to decorate papier mâché as long as the resulting colour and pattern is sealed using PVA or white glue (which dries clear) as a varnish. Finally, you can embellish your papier mâché pieces with old buttons, beads, stickers, studs, shells or droplet stones, all of which add interest and colour.

Previous pages: This collection of decorative papier mâché jewellery was made by layering paper to build up strong, sculptural shapes. Each piece is then painted in a range of subtle, organic tones.
(Julia Manheim)

Right: The advantage of papier mâché for earrings is that you can design large, dramatic pieces that are light and comfortable to wear. An ideal choice for beginners, papier mâché is inexpensive and easy to use.
(Marion Elliot)

until you have covered them with roughly one layer and they resemble neat parcels. Make sure that the sides of each shape retain their edges because these emphasize their three-dimensional effect. Leave the covered shapes to dry.

6 *Once the shapes are thoroughly dry, apply the first base coat of paint. Use a white base coat on both sides of each shape and leave to dry. Check the drying times; for enamel paint allow six hours. Next, paint your chosen design onto all the shapes and leave to dry. Once dry, protect the finished design with a thin layer of PVA or white glue which acts as sealant and varnish and strengthens the surface.*

7 *In order to create the holes to thread the jump rings onto, simply take a sharp compass point and gently but firmly pierce*

the papier mâché shapes from one side to the other. You can then link both shapes together using a jump ring. To link the heart shape to the lower section pierce a hole in each shape at the edge section where the two shapes dovetail. Thread a jump ring through each hole and close tightly with pliers.

8 *Measure and pierce three separate holes in the edge of each lower suspended section. Next, take three jump rings, link them (see p.25) to the three glass drops, then thread the rings through the holes at the edge of the suspended lower section and close the links tightly with pliers. This forms the bead fringe. Finally, turn each fully assembled earring over and glue an earring finding onto the reverse of the top heart section with an epoxy glue. Leave to dry.*

The flexibility of "soft" jewellery components like fabric and leather makes them particularly well-suited to the concept of "body sculpture" as they can be moulded to fit the contours of the body. Many decorative finishes can be applied to fabric and leather to give them definition and interest. For example, padding or quilting will give a piece extra dimensions, while patchwork or collage will introduce contrast into a design. One of the beauties of fabric jewellery is the ease with which it moves over the garments it dresses. However, in order to make the best possible use of a fabric, it is important that you understand its natural properties. For example, with the right handling, you can successfully emphasize the natural grain and colouring of a fabric, while you can create contrasts

and decorated with seed beads and the hair of a monkey.

There are a huge variety of soft jewellery materials to choose from, including rubber, yarn, feathers, felt, fake fur and even horsehair. You can buy most of these from craft stores, although you may be able to find fabric scraps around the home. A further source of fabrics such as lace or net is antique shops or fairs, while feathers are usually available from aviaries.

Using fabrics

Techniques compatible with fabric include embroidery, knitting, macramé, patchwork and appliqué. And you can use applied decoration such as beading or studding to transform a plain piece of fabric into a decorative ornament.

You can easily adapt the decorative art of appliqué,

Previous page left to right: Fabric hoop earrings and curled leather cuff (Michael de Nardo); pleated fan brooch (Ruth Elliott and Gail de Jong); black and white tweed earrings (Eric Beamon); embroidered cameo brooch (Linda Miller); horsehair necklace (Daphne Shepherd); rubber bracelet (Mandy Nash); silk earclips (Frannie); bead and plaited embroidery thread necklace (Katrina Smith);

fabric & leather

through combining different textures. Although soft jewellery does not have a long history, many of its associated techniques, such as stringing and beading, are recognized crafts that have been practised for thousands of years. If anything, fabric jewellery is making history now, as designers explore new and exciting techniques. The trend for using fabric for jewellery was first manifested in large neck pieces. In the 1940s, fluid jewellery shapes in draped velvets and silks became popular and even glass and paste jewellery began to imitate the textures and folds of fabric.

Soft jewellery is an important medium that is worth considering if you want to take inspiration from ethnic cultures that use natural fibres and skins for adornment. For instance, an African neckpiece currently in the U.C.L.A. in the United States, is made from goat skin

which involves the application of one piece of material to another, to make fabric jewellery. The appliquéd components, which range from satin ribbons to leather strips, must be compatible with the fabric that they are decorating in terms of weight and appearance. And you should make sure that you use a strong enough base material to support the appliqué without tearing. Annie and Giuliano Sereni of Sheer Decadence use appliqué to mount glass and plastic beads onto stiffened rayon, silk and satin. They either keep the fabric flat in a collage effect or bunch it with beads which they insert into the folds. Their jewellery, which ranges from sculptural v-shaped necklaces to elaborate earrings and brooches, is inspired by the Renaissance and is often decorated with elaborate beadwork which they suspend from the base of their pieces.

gold braid and brass brooch (Judy Clayton); leather necklace (Glenis Howshall); black cowl decorated with ribbons (Susie Freeman); antique brocade medal (Eric Rhein); fabric and bead hair comb (Sheer Decadence); fleece bead choker (Victoria Brown); gold leather crown earrings (Glenis Howshall); embroidered earrings (Janice Gilmore).

Opposite: Decorated voile neck cowls (Susie Freeman).

A technique more usually associated with dressmaking, embroidery is equally effective when applied to fabric jewellery. A stiff material forms a good base and you can achieve interesting finishes by working unusual threads and even beads and sequins into your design. Linda Miller machine-embroiders onto heavyweight untreated calico with rayon thread from Germany and India. Using a free embroidery technique, she works mainly on figurative and mythical designs. Once she has completed her design, she cuts the embroidered fabric into shape and neatens the edges with zig-zag stitch. This is designed to stiffen the calico so that it is strong enough to be worn as hairslides, brooches, earrings and cuff links.

Painting, printing and dyeing fabric

Colour is an important factor in soft jewellery design. If you can't find a fabric in a suitable natural tone, you can always dye a piece yourself. Tie-dyeing involves the immersion of fabric in a dye bath (a large basin). First, fold the areas to be protected and tie them with cord or elastic bands (if you like, you can fill the bunches with small stones or rice). Following the dye manufacturer's instructions, immerse the prepared cloth in a dye bath. For a multi-coloured finish, repeat the dyeing process using a different coloured dye each time. Batik allows for more pattern control than tie-dyeing, as the protected areas are painted with hot wax before immersion. And you can hand-print fabric at home using ink in conjunction with anything from etched potatoes to sponges. Dating back to the 17th century, silkscreen printing is one of the most popular printing processes. First, selected areas of a piece of silk fabric are blocked and coated with melted wax or gum which is applied using a brush or sponge. Then the piece of silk is stretched over a frame, to form a screen, and ink is passed through the unprotected areas of the screen and onto the fabric.

Judy Clayton has developed her own methods for hand-painting silk which she then moulds into flat or three-dimensional jewellery shapes. She lays out the silk and thread in a collage format and covers them with transparent plastic. Then she randomly machine-stitches this collage into place and shrinks it in hot water. Finally, she embellishes the resulting curled shapes with embroidery or decorates them with beads.

Using thread

Yarn, thread, cord or rope are frequently used in fabric jewellery and are available in a wide choice of colours from department stores. The coarseness or smoothness of a thread will dictate the ways in which you can use it – it can be knitted, crocheted or knotted to form sturdy foundations or decorations for jewellery.

Stitching onto fabric has structural, as well as decorative functions – you can build up several layers with elaborate machine stitches. Hand-stitching is often quite effective in providing a bolder, more random pattern, while you can create contrasting designs by fitting fabric shapes together in a patchwork collage and securing them with a cross or zig-zag stitch.

Based on a series of chain stitches, crochet techniques can be used to create intricate patterns in three dimensions. You can stuff, wrap or appliqué crocheted work in the same way as most fabrics and it is delicate enough to make into small items of jewellery. Weaving has many decorative possibilities too. It is even possible to thread beads and sequins onto the warp thread and incorporate them into your design.

Macramé is a knotting technique that requires no specialized tools. Its intricacy depends on the variety of knots you use, although beginners should keep these simple. Macramé knots serve many purposes other than as pure decoration – you can use a square knot to fasten, add texture or create a three-dimensional structure. You can embellish macramé with tassels or fringes or thread your pieces with bells or beads.

Wrapping involves binding thread or rope around a central core shape. Katrina Smith uses this technique to twist her own machine-embroidered cord or chenille

Above: The sunflower-shaped brooch in iridescent mauves and pinks is fashioned from beaten brass and has a string of beads and a brass spiral suspended from its base. The intricate central design detail is created by machine-embroidering silk fabrics and threads into place. (Judy Clayton)

wool around natural materials, such as shells, chestnuts, hazelnuts and dried wood. Her colourful, chunky pieces are influenced by African tribal rituals and body painting. Sometimes she leaves the natural base of a piece exposed – for example, a barnacle shell has its hollow revealed and is filled with glass or wood beads.

Using hair

The trend for hair jewellery, especially popular in France during the 1840s and 1850s, evolved from Victorian mourning jewellery when locks of hair were arranged as weeping willows (see p.15). Human hair was also considered as a love token and hair was often plaited or woven into bracelets which were studded with gemstones or precious metals. However, horsehair soon surpassed human hair in popularity as it was easier to work and could be dyed, bleached, wound into discs or mounted in bracelets or brooches. Horsehair has a higher lustre than wool, but is difficult to braid because it is so brittle. For this reason, it is best kept wet during the working process. Another disadvantage is that horsehair is inconsistent in length and thickness. Daphne Shepherd uses horsehair to great effect for her openwork necklace and bracelet designs (see p.68).

Using leather

Leather is an increasingly popular medium for jewellery and is available in many grades, ranging from soft suede, calf and nappa (kid's leather) to heavier cow hide. Soft leathers are particularly suitable for appliqué and patchwork as they are malleable and easy to cut, while heavy leathers are not as versatile (especially when working with small pieces of jewellery). To work heavy leather you need a sharp craft knife and an appropriate glue (gluing is preferable to stitching). You can stitch leather by hand or machine, using a strong silk or synthetic sewing thread and a special leather needle. Saddler's thread or leather thonging is ideal for constructing sturdier pieces, while buttonhole silk thread is best for fine leather. Some leathers have natural heavily textured patterns which can be incorporated into the design, but if you want to decorate a piece with embossed or stamped designs, it is best to work with ungrained leather. You can inlay eyelets and stones into leather with an epoxy resin. Some leathers, mainly vegetable-tanned hides, are mouldable when wet and retain their shapes when dry. You can either stretch leather by hand, or work a piece into a three-dimensional shape by soaking the leather in water, wrapping it around an object such as a rolling pin or bottle and leaving it to dry.

Leather can be finished in many ways. It can be antiqued, where the surface is sprayed to produce irregular shading, shaped or embossed with metal dies. It can be coated with Dutch metal or foil, patented with lacquers and varnishes or pearlized. While you should avoid dyeing suede, you can colour most leathers using special leather dye, which is applied with a soft cloth or brush, or acrylic paints, available in a range of opaque and transparent colours, which maintain their elasticity. Marker pens can be used to colour suede, as can stencilling techniques.

Glenis Howshall creates ornamental, three-dimensional shapes by wrapping leather around a wire armature, gluing it in place and decorating it with beads and precious stones. Flat leather pieces are spiralled, twisted and zig-zagged into largely geometrical shapes. Glenis works with pre-coloured leather which she sometimes coats with metallic paint to imitate precious metals. She often covers the findings, which are integral to her jewellery, with leather.

Soft jewellery encompasses a wide range of materials, both synthetic and natural, most of which are easy to work with and comfortable to wear. Often the most attractive jewellery relies on the natural grain and pattern of the material it is made from and requires very little additional embellishment. For example, peacock feathers create drama by themselves, while the natural grain of some leathers would be lost if they were artificially coloured or embossed.

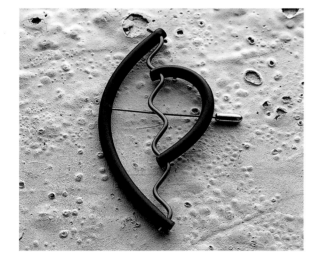

Above: Contemporary designers use a wealth of unorthodox materials to produce unique items of jewellery like this bizarre brooch, which has been fashioned from two lengths of black rubber tubing and a piece of blue twisted oxidized aluminium piping. (Mandy Nash)

how to **s**tiffen **f**abric

Equipment and materials

12in (30cm) muslin fabric

Casting resin or PVA (white) glue

Hardener

Gold paint

Liquid fabric paint

Glaze or varnish

Ballpoint pen

Cardboard

Paper

Scissors

Adhesive tape or staples

Dressmakers' pins

Household iron

Dish or shallow receptacle

Releasing agent (petroleum jelly)

Knife

Assorted paint brushes including a 1½-in (4-cm) bristle brush

Tape measure

Household gloves

This bracelet looks soft and pliable, but is in fact rigid and hard-wearing. Its inspirations are the romantic, rococo looks of draped, folded and rippled fabrics. It is highlighted by subtle gilding which catches the relief texture and gives the bracelet a rich, antiqued look.

The bangle in the illustration is designed to fit tightly around the wrist but you may prefer to make a wider armlet to fit around your upper arm.

Immersing the fabric in resin reinforces the muslin, enabling you to drape it in folds which will give the bracelet a textured look. Casting resin is simple to use, providing you follow the manufacturer's instructions and take the appropriate safety precautions (see p.98). Make sure that you work in a well-ventilated room (avoid smoking and take care not to inhale toxic fumes) and avoid getting resin on your skin – if you suffer from

1 *To determine the size of your bangle, take a tape measure and wind it around the circumference of your wrist. On a piece of cardboard, draw a rectangle 12in (30cm) wide and the length of your wrist. Bend the cardboard shape to form a tube of the same dimensions as your wrist. Fix the ends together with strong adhesive tape and staples. This tube will serve as a base mould to support the bound fabric while it is drying.*

2 *Fold the piece of muslin in half lengthways to form two layers – this will help to stiffen the bracelet. Using a ballpoint pen, draw a rectangle 5½in (14cm) wide and twice the length of your wrist onto a piece of paper to form a template. (The wrist length is doubled to allow for the tied knot which forms the*

central design detail.) Pin the paper template onto the double-thickness muslin and cut out the rectangular shape with scissors. Remove the paper pattern and fold the muslin in half again lengthways to form four layers.

3 *Neaten the raw edges of the fabric by turning under a few millimetres of the folded fabric. Iron this neatened edge in place to make it crisp and permanent.*

4 *In a shallow dish, make up a small quantity of resin according to the supplier's instructions. Add the corresponding number of drops of hardener and stir the mixture thoroughly with the end of a paint brush. Wearing household gloves, submerge the strip of muslin in the resin in sections, making*

sensitive skin, it is a good idea to apply a barrier cream to your hands.

Gold paint, which is used to embellish the bangle, is available in liquid form in small bottles from art supply stores (see p.140). Apply this sparingly to the painted bangle using a broad bristle brush of about the same width as the bracelet. Although it is more effective to leave the bracelet matte, you could varnish it if you wish.

Right: This seemingly soft- and fragile-looking knotted bracelet is made up of layers of muslin fabric which have been stiffened by immersing them in casting resin. After building the resinous fabric around a mould, it is left to set and the resulting solid shape is finally hand-painted and gilded to achieve a burnished, antiqued and textured effect.
(Gail de Jong and Ruth Elliott)

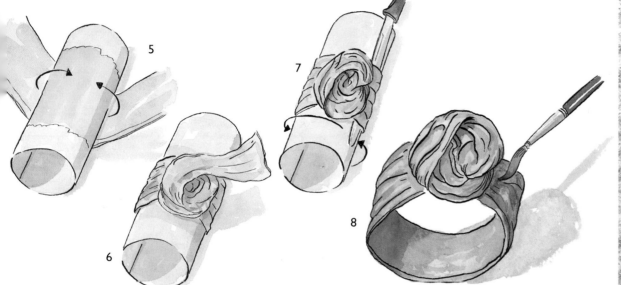

sure that the resin is evenly distributed throughout. Work quickly and carefully as the resin will only remain workable at room temperature for about 20 minutes.

5 *Smear the cardboard mould with the releasing agent to prevent the resin-treated fabric from sticking to it when it is left to set. As you wrap the length of impregnated fabric around the tube, manipulate the muslin into folds and ripples to give the bracelet a textured effect. Once ruched, the band should be 1½in (4cm) wide.*

6 *To form the central knotted design detail, tie the double ends of the fabric together to form a knot, or you may prefer to twist them tightly together to form a simulated knot. Neaten any*

loose ends by tucking them unobtrusively within the knot.

7 *Leave the bracelet to dry. When it has almost set, gently slide a knife between the tube and the bracelet to loosen it. Don't remove the cardboard tube at this stage – it is easier to remove after the resin hardens. Leave the bracelet in a warm place for 24 hours until it has set as hard as leather, then remove the cardboard tube. If the bracelet is still flimsy at this stage, paint another layer of resin, or a resin-based filler, around the inside of the bracelet with a paint brush.*

8 *When the bracelet is thoroughly set, paint it in your chosen colour and leave it to dry. Finally, gild it sparingly with gold paint. Once dry, either varnish or simply leave matte.*

how to make **fl**eece **b**eads

Equipment and materials

Raw sheep's fleece

Assortment of acid or
domestic dyes

Household soap or
soap flakes

Large embroidery
needle or bodkin

Strong thread

Assorted glass beads
and sequins

Short head pins

Discharge paste

Good-quality glue
suitable for use on
fabrics

Scissors

Scalpel or craft knife

Cocktail (swizzle) stick

Dry foam flower-
arranging block

These beads look like they have been made from felt, but in fact they are crafted from raw sheep's fleece. This is torn into small sections, washed in hot, soapy water and then fashioned into a tightly compacted ball of woollen fibres. The heat from the water and the agitating process cause the fibres to mat together and form a hard ball. The beads can then be dyed individually or, if you are dying lots of beads the same colour, you may prefer to dye the fleece in its raw state before you make it into balls. (If you decide to dye the fleece beforehand, make sure that you use a colour-fast dye.) Once these processes are complete, you can decorate the beads with sequins, rocaille beads or discharge paste or you could create two-tone beads by gluing two different-coloured bead halves together.

Although fleece can be purchased from craft and specialist wool shops, if you are visiting the countryside you may be able to obtain raw sheep's fleece, in its natural form, from a local farmer. You can colour fleece with acid or domestic dyes which are available in a wide

1 *Wash the raw fleece by immersing it in a tub of hot, soapy water. Rinse the fleece thoroughly in clean water then squeeze out the excess. Divide the fleece into sections and, following the manufacturer's instructions, dye them in your chosen colours.*

2 *Tear a small bundle of wool from the cleaned and dyed fleece and place it in hot, soapy water. Using your hands, squeeze, compress and roll the clump of wool into a solid mass. Continue to do this for about 30 minutes or until the wool shrinks and compresses into a hard ball.*

3 *Place the wool ball in another tub of hot water and squeeze out the remaining soap. (The bead should now retain its*

spherical shape perfectly.) Leave the bead in a warm, dry place for 24 hours or until it has dried thoroughly. Make up some more beads in the same way, varying the size of the beads by using different quantities of fleece.

4 *You can either decorate the fleece beads or simply leave them plain. Decorate some beads with polka dots by applying discharge paste with a small paint brush in your desired pattern. To support the bead while you are decorating it, stab it with a cocktail (swizzle) stick and place one end of the stick in a piece of flower-arranger's foam.*

5 *For a different effect, thread rocaille beads onto short head*

range of colours. Domestic dyes are available from hardware shops and department stores, but if you decide to work with acid dyes, you may need to purchase them from a specialist craft store.

The fleece beads in the illustration have been strung, using a large needle, onto strong thread to form a necklace. However, you could thread them onto elastic to create a bracelet or you could make a pair of earrings by cutting a ball in half with a craft knife and gluing each half onto an earring finding clip.

Previous pages: A colourful array of woollen beaded necklaces and bracelets. Each bead is formed by hand from natural sheep's fleece, which is then dyed, hand-painted and sometimes embellished with pins, small beads and sequins.
(Victoria Brown)

Right: Once you have mastered the art of making and dyeing circular fleece beads, you can experiment with different shapes and sizes or even glue two different-coloured halves together to create a two-tone bead effect.
(Victoria Brown)

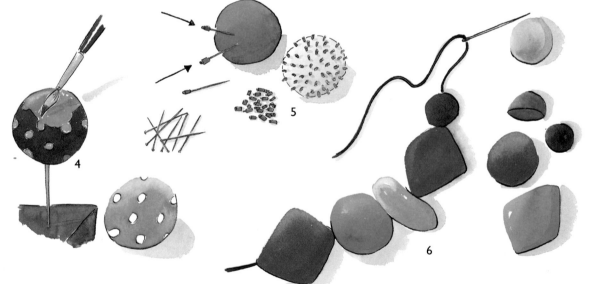

pins, apply a little glue to the blunt end and puncture the fleece bead all over with them, rather like a pin cushion.

To make two-tone beads, cut two different-coloured balls in half with a craft knife or scalpel. Apply a good-quality glue, suitable for fabrics, to the cross-sections of the two different-coloured halves and sandwich them together.

6 *To make the fleece beads into a necklace, take a length of strong thread (nylon thread is ideal) and a large needle or bodkin, tie a knot toward the end of the thread and pass the needle through the middle of the fleece bead. You can either string the beads simply, or string and knot them.*

To produce a knotted string, press the bead against the first knot, form a loop on the other side of the bead, ease the new loop into a knot by pushing it toward the bead with the tip of the needle and pulling the thread tight – this will hold the bead in place. Continue threading and knotting the fleece beads in this way until you have achieved the length you require for your necklace (see pages 31 and 32 for standard necklace lengths). Secure the ends of the thread with a double knot. Cut off the excess thread with a pair of scissors and conceal the ends by threading them onto a needle and passing this through the middle of the final bead.

Although many of the materials used for contemporary jewellery-making are new and revolutionary, the art of metalwork often follows the basic rules set out by early craftsmen thousands of years ago. Apart from the advent of electroplating in the 19th century and the more efficient techniques allowed by today's machines, many of the basic metalworking principles remain unchanged. Before they became a fashion accessory, metal and jewels served a more symbolic function – they were usually worn as talismans or amulets to fend off evil spirits, as in Egypt, where tomb jewellery not only signified status, but was also used to adorn the dead.

Metals are chemical or mineral substances that are

Pure gold is known as proof gold or fine gold, but because it is too soft for jewellery in its natural form it is usually alloyed with silver and copper to produce a more workable material. Gold solder is normally made up of the same amount of gold, but it is alloyed to metal which allows it to melt at a lower temperature. The proportion of alloy determines the colour of gold – which can be classified as yellow, green, red or white – and also its carat (karat) value (pure gold is 24 carat).

Fine silver is the purest of silvers, while its hardened form, sterling, is the most popular for jewellery use. This contains 92.5 percent silver to 7.5 percent copper. Both types are available in many forms, including bar, powder, sheet and rod. Other silvers occasionally used

Previous page left to right: Drop earrings bound with Indian brass wire (Glynneth Barren); verdigris necklace decorated with clubs, hearts and spades (Jenifer Corker); cast pewter necklace with enamelled decoration (Louise Nagle); embossed metal brooch and earring (Julia Foster); knitted copper wire cuff (Emma Clegg); coiled oxidized metal brooch with green beads (Yukatek);

metal

mined in their natural or pure state, often occurring as ores. The word "metal" comes from the Greek "metallon", meaning metal or mine, and today metals are mined all over the world. Metals are malleable in their solid state and are good heat conductors, but for most jewellery processes they need to be refined and cast into ingots before use.

Metals are divided into non-ferrous and ferrous categories. Ferrous metals, such as steel, contain iron and alloys, while non-ferous metals are precious or base. The three precious or noble metals are gold, silver and platinum (these are most commonly used for jewellery-making), while base metals include aluminium, copper, lead, nickel and tin.

for jewellery are Britannia silver, coin silver and continental silver – this is mostly used in Europe. Silver solders are mainly alloys of silver and copper.

Platinum was first introduced to Europe from South America in 1741. The name "platinum" covers a group of metals arranged in three pairs. The most important for jewellery-making are platinum and palladium, both sourced in Canada. Platinum is highly resistant to corrosion and oxidization and is often used for diamond settings. Its melting point is a lot higher than other metals, as are its solders, which are white in colour.

Precious metals were first imported in large quantities to the West during the 15th century, at which time jewellery became more fashionable. New technical

rosette brooch (Sue Horth); star-shaped dangle earring (Mary Farrell); eyelash earring with turquoise stone and coiled gold-plated cuff (Van der Straeten); icicle drop earring (Mary Farrell); twisted wire necklace (Yukatek).

Opposite: Embossed and acid-etched jewellery depicting Old Testament texts. (Julia Foster)

innovations emerged and surface finishes, such as enamel, came into their own. Metal jewellery became available to a wider market during the Industrial Revolution, when production spread to the steel and iron industries. During the 19th century, cut steel jewellery became popular and this period saw the introduction of Berlin Ironwork, which made use of *repoussé* methods.

Electroplating revolutionized metal- and jewellery-making during the 1940s. This finish involved covering the surface of an object with a film of gold or silver, so that it imitated the real thing. After World War II, interest in contemporary metal jewellery snowballed and today its popularity remains as strong as ever.

Soldering

This process involves joining two pieces of metal together by applying solder and heat to the joint. The solder alloy is usually comprised of the metal to be soldered along with additional metals; it is a permanent filler and has a lower melting point than the metals being joined. Each precious metal has a corresponding range of suitable solders. Hard solder melts at a higher temperature than medium solder, while soft solder is used for metals with low-melting points.

Solders are available from jewellery suppliers. Basic soldering tools are solder snips for cutting the solder, tweezers, clamps (for holding the metal pieces in place) and a soldering block or fire brick. You will also need flux, such as borax, which you apply to the joints to aid the flow of the solder. (When the metal is heated, an element called oxide builts up on its surface and flux prevents this from inhibiting the join.) There are various types of flux on the market and these must be chosen in relation to the metal being used – for example, a paste flux, which fuses at high temperatures, is ideal for gold. Before you begin soldering, make sure that you file the joints so that they fit together and clean the two metal surfaces to be joined with steel wool. The soldering process involves applying heat to the surrounding metals with an oxidizing flame, usually from a blow torch. When you have heated the metal sufficiently, apply the flame to the joint and solder, working in a circular motion. The flux will bubble and turn white, then it will darken and the solder will melt and run along the join. Switch off the flame when the solder completely fills the joint. Next, clean the metal in a pickling solution (see p.85).

Casting

There are various techniques for transforming metals into shapes. Casting is one such technique and involves pouring molten metal into a mould or crucible where it is left to harden. This technique was first mastered in Mesopotamia more than 5,000 years ago, when moulds were chiselled from stone or baked clay and filled with molten metal. Craftsmen later developed the piece mould, a familiar object among contemporary jewellers, which was followed by the more sophisticated lost wax method, or *Cire Perdue*, which involved modelling an object in wax, then coating it in clay.

Depending on the melting temperature of the metal being cast, metal can either be melted with a blow torch (for low-melting metals) or in a kiln (for high-melting metals). While high-melting techniques are complex and should be undertaken by a skilled jeweller, soft-melting can be carried out in the home by a beginner. Louise Nagle constructs her moulds from cuttle-fish bones which give her pieces a textured finish (see p.112).

Annealing

The Bronze Age saw the discovery of many metalwork techniques which are still in use today. Annealing, a process that restores the flexibility of a metal after it has been hardened by hammering, was an important discovery made by ancient goldsmiths. It involves heating the metal above its specific annealing temperature. This transforms the metal's grain structure and makes the metal soft. The metal is brushed with flux and heated with a soft flame over its entire surface. The metal will harden and go rigid as it cools, so once

Above: This dangle earring is fashioned from galvanized wire which is spiralled into a pod shape and coloured using acrylic paint. The irregular bead shape inside the wire cage is made from cork which is hand-painted in many colours with the same acrylic paint. (Yukatek)

the hammer starts to spring back, use the blow torch to reheat the metal's surface.

Metal can also be cut into a shape, but before you start cutting, make sure that you measure and mark your design. Steel rulers are designed for this, while protractors or spring dividers are used for angles and circles. Cutting techniques include drilling, sawing and chiselling, while shearing, the most basic method, can be carried out using scissors, hand shears or tin snips.

Pickling

After heat treatments such as soldering, annealing and casting, you should chemically clean the metals in a pickling solution. Pickle is an acid solution into which the metal is immersed to remove firescale (surface soil) and firestain (soil below the surface). Pickling also cleans away surplus flux and carbon deposits, but you must first manually clean the surface of the metal with abrasive paper and rub the joints with steel wool. Pickling solutions were traditionally made from organic acids such as citric acid, but today mineral acids, like nitric, sulphuric and hydrochloric acid, are used. These are highly corrosive and should be stored out of the reach of children. Alum is perhaps the most common pickling solution and this is safe to use at home. Simply place your piece of jewellery in a heat-resistant container with the alum and heat gently over the stove.

Decorating metal

As well as the actual working and moulding of metal, metal decoration is of equal historic importance. There are various methods for making a design on metal. *Repoussage*, which literally means "to push again", and chasing are both techniques for embossing metal with different-shaped punches. *Repoussage* indicates that the metal was hammered both from the front and from the reverse side, while chasing refers to a design punched into the front. Stamping is an ancient method for embossing an impression into metal with a stamping punch. Engraving, the art of carving incisions into metal, was employed in Egypt as early as 2,000BC.

The art of inlaying one metal into another metal to develop a contrasting colour, was perfected in Japan, where it was used to decorate Samurai swords.

Embossing and stamping techniques are widely used to decorate metal beads. Asia, Turkey and India have long traditions of producing highly decorated beads with relief designs. Woven metal beads are produced in the Philippines, while in Africa, jewellers make metal beads from recycled saucepans, coins and auto parts.

Metal wire is another important medium in jewellery-making. The wire is "drawn" into the required thickness by pulling it through a draw plate. Once it is the right diameter, the wire can be twisted, spiralled or worked into the ancient and delicate art of filigree.

Emma Clegg uses an old domestic knitting machine to knit fine copper wire into lively shapes. She uses electrical wire for her pieces, which is available in brown, red and gold colours and unlike silver wire, which she has experimented with, is not prone to snapping. After knitting, Emma folds the knitted length into a shape, threads it with beads and finally varnishes it (see p.80).

While it is possible to colour metals with chemicals, this is a complex and lengthy process and should only be undertaken by a skilled craftsman. Jenifer Corker, who uses chemicals to achieve a dramatic verdigris colour, warns that it is a "temperamental process".

The final stage for making metal jewellery is polishing and buffing. First, remove any scratches with graded emery paper, then apply tripoli polish with an electric mop to achieve a good finish. Clean the piece thoroughly in hot, soapy water to remove any residual polish, then apply jeweller's rouge, clean off and dry.

Although the technical details in this chapter may seem awesome to the beginner, with practice you should soon feel confident enough to carry out many of the metalworking processes yourself. However, for those of you who are not convinced, you can always entrust your pieces to a specialist craftsman who will carry out the trickiest operations for you.

Above: This rosette brooch demonstrates how you can create beautiful jewellery from mundane objects. For example, the fine wire mesh which this brooch is made from is used to make air vents. After setting in resin, it is coloured in burnished browns and golds.
(Sue Horth)

how to **b**ind and **c**oil **s**ilver **w**ire

Equipment and materials

.

Spool of 4-mm fine-gauge silver-plated wire

Spool of 6-mm thick-gauge silver-plated wire

End cutters

Epoxy glue or soldering iron

Vice

2 earclip findings

Mary Farrell was inspired to make three-dimensional wire jewellery after working with paper on a wire base. She bases her jewellery on bizarre architectural forms and animation imagery. Mary does not draw the design first, but claims that the more you work in this medium, the more you visualize the result.

Before you begin to construct the earrings, you must first choose the shape you want – in this case a nine-point sunburst which encircles a spiral disc. The earrings are constructed by making a flat skeleton or armature from thick-gauge silver-plated wire. The other layers are then bound onto the armature by hand using a fine-gauge silver-plated wire. Finally, the central dome of spirally bound wire is coiled by hand onto a flat coiled wire spiral which is the working base of the sunburst design.

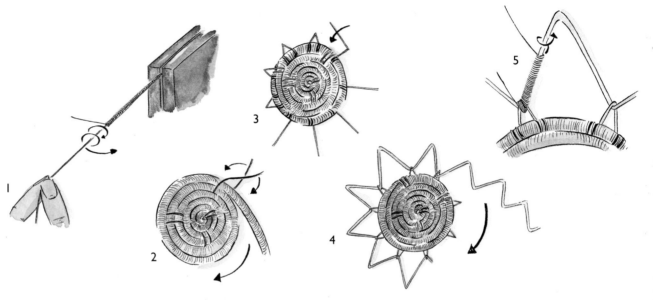

1 *Take a piece of thick-gauge wire measuring 9½in (24cm) long. Place one end in a vice and hold the other end firmly between your fingers. Take a 12-in (30-cm) length of fine-gauge wire and tightly bind this wire around the entire length of the thick-gauge wire. Bind uniformly without overlapping and let each preceding bind of wire guide the next. Continue in this manner until the whole length of thick wire is completely hidden by the fine wire. Snip off the excess with end cutters.*

2 *Lay this wrapped wire on a flat surface and coil it into a small, flat spiral disc. Bind each turn of the wire to the next with a piece of fine-gauge wire to secure and retain the developing shape. Do this unobtrusively at five or six intervals. Snip off the excess.*

3 *To construct the nine-pointed fins which form the sunburst shape, measure accurately nine equal points around the circumference of the spiral. Mark each of these points with 2-in (5-cm) lengths of fine-gauge wire. Secure each length of wire by winding one end tightly around the outer row of the spiral. Bend each 2-in (5-cm) wire in half and secure the end by winding it tightly a couple of times around the outer coil of the spiral disc. Clip off excess with end cutters and secure the sharp end by weaving it into the the outer coil of the spiral. Then take a 9½-in (24-cm) length of thick-gauge wire and bend it at ½in (1.3cm) intervals to form nine equal zig-zag points.*

4 *To attach this zig-zag length to the nine wire-marked points, take fine silver wire, secure one end by twisting it*

Silver-plated wire is available in various degrees or gauges of thickness and quality. Always work with surplus wire to your requirements, because if you underestimate the quantity of wire, you will have to bind a new joint which you will not be able to render invisible. You can remove any residual wire by simply clipping it off with end cutters when you have completed each section satisfactorily.

Previous pages: A selection of silver-plated wire jewellery embellished with marbles, including a pendulum earring and matching starburst necklace and a gold lacquered brooch. (Mary Farrell)

Right: A pair of intricately shaped, three-dimensional earrings, structured from thick- and fine-gauge silver-plated wire which has been coiled into a nine-point sunburst shape. (Mary Farrell)

around a marker and bind diagonally around one of the markers. Place the zig-zag length so its lower points intersect with the upper points of the wire markers.

5 *Next, bind a length of fine wire around the first diagonal of the fin from bottom to top.*

6 *Then bind this fine wire horizontally across the triangle, starting at the top point. Bind tightly and uniformly, making sure that the wire is parallel and evenly distributed across the triangle armature. When you reach the double stump formed by the marker wire at the base, twist the binding wire around the stump, then take the wire across to the next empty segment.*

7 *Bind the wire straight up the diagonal to the highest point of the adjacent triangle and repeat the horizontal binding*

technique. Continue in this way until all the triangle segments are bound with silver-plated wire.

8 *To build the central pod in the middle of the earring, bind a length of thick-gauge wire with fine silver wire, using the same method as for step 1. Wind one end of the wire securely around the edge of the central spiral disc. Coil the wire around the periphery of the spiral and build on top of the first row, securing at intervals as you did for the original base coil. (Imagine the structure of a vase fashioned from a continuous thin sausage of clay.) When you reach a height of ½in (1.25cm), graduate the wire into the middle, spiralling to form a cap. Bind each turn to the next with fine-gauge wire as for step 2. Glue or solder an earclip finding to the back.*

how to **a**nneal **m**etal

Equipment and materials

16in x 32in (20cm x 40cm) thin brass or copper metal sheeting

Large quantity of thick, heavy, copper jump rings

7 cabochon semi-precious stones

T-bar attachment and ring fastening

Piercing saw

Fine drill

Blow torch

Fire brick or steel block

Steel tweezers

Steel textured hammer

Scriber

Fine metal file

Jeweller's soldering wig

Basic workbench with peg attachment

Silver and lead solder

Soldering iron

Flux

Paint brush

Round-nosed pliers

Protective gloves

This bracelet has a deliberately hand-finished, beaten appearance, designed to represent a find from Ancient Egypt. The designers employed soldering, annealing and planishing techniques to make the piece. (Planishing involves hammering metal to give it a final finish.) To help with the soldering process, the designers used a jeweller's soldering wig – a circular mat of twisted iron wire with a handle. This is an indispensable tool when soldering small pieces of metal as the wires can be twisted around your piece of work to support it. The jeweller's wig allows a minimum of heat dispersion, so you can heat a piece of metal to an even temperature. Once you have constructed the bracelet, you could have it plated in gold by a specialist plater (see p.140).

If the metalwork processes are too complicated for you, you could achieve a similar effect by finding and

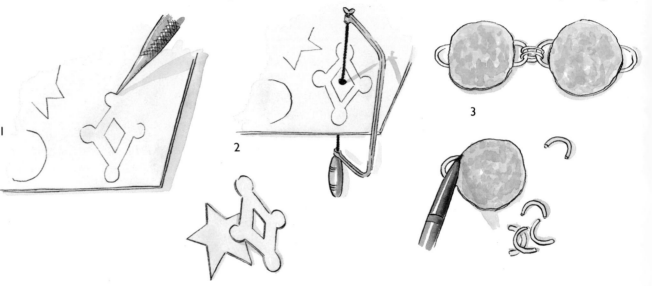

1 *Put the brass or copper sheeting on the bench peg. Using a scriber, draw five irregular-shaped metal discs ³/₄in (2cm) in diameter, three irregular-shaped metal discs 1in (2.5cm) in diameter and seven five-point star settings for cabochon stones (see how to mount a stone, steps 1 & 2, p.120).*

2 *Clamp the shapes in the bench peg and cut each shape out with a piercing saw. To make the three cross-shaped charms, draw an outer shape 1in x 1¹/₂in (2.5cm x 4cm), pierce the middle with a fine drill, insert the saw blade through the hole and carefully cut out a central diamond shape. To create the rippled and beaten texture, hold a shape in a pair of steel tweezers over a steel block or fire brick and use the blow torch to apply heat to the entire surface. When the shape is red-hot, put*

it on the steel block or fire brick and beat it vigorously with a steel textured hammer to achieve an uneven finish. Repeat this annealing process for each of the 15 shapes.

3 *While the shapes are cooling, take five large jump rings and cut them in half using a piercing saw. The 10 resulting crescent-shaped links will be soldered either side of the five ³/₄-in (2-cm) discs, which will then be linked together with jump rings to form the main bracelet length. To solder these half jump rings to the five discs, support a half jump ring in the jeweller's wig ready for soldering. Switch the soldering iron on. Using a small brush, paint a little flux over the outer edge of a ³/₄-in (2-cm) disc. Unwind some silver solder from the roll. Touch the tip of the solder with the tip of the soldering iron – a small amount of*

using hammered and drilled coins or buttons, large threaded bellcaps enclosing a large bead or even costume jewellery rings linked to a jump ring.

The designers of this bracelet linked the large metal discs, cabochon stones and cross shapes to the main bracelet with chains made up from a varied number of thick, heavy-weight jump rings, which helps to achieve a random and irregular look.

Previous pages: This gold-plated collection includes a necklace of gold-plated discs with suspended acrylic stones, a coiled spiral bracelet and a curled gold-plated earring.
(Van der Straeten)

Right: A chunky gold-plated charm bracelet made from beaten metal discs linked with jump rings. The moss-agate and amethyst cabochon stones are set in drop claw settings.
(Van der Straeten)

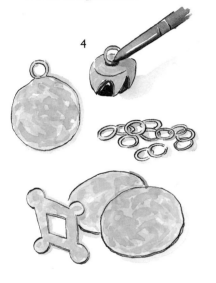

the solder should adhere to the iron (if it does not, allow more time for the soldering iron to heat). Next, touch the two tips of the jump ring with the tip of the soldering iron – a little molten solder should adhere. Press the side of the metal disc against the solder-coated half jump ring and hold the disc in place with tweezers until it adheres. Attach a half jump ring to the opposite side of the disc in the same manner. Repeat this process for each of the five brass or copper discs.

Link the five metal discs together with five pairs of jump rings (see p.25). Open up the join in each ring with pliers. Thread the jump ring through two of the soldered half jump rings. Squeeze the join in the jump ring tightly shut with pliers. Link the same discs with a second jump ring in the same way.

Continue in this manner until all five metal discs are linked together with a pair of jump rings.

4 *Mount the seven cabochon stones in five-point star settings (see how to mount a stone, steps 3-5, p.120). Using lead solder, solder a jump ring onto the base of each mounted stone using the method described in step 3.*

5 *Attach the T-bar to one end of the bracelet and the ring fastening to the other end with jump rings.*

Solder a half-jump ring to each of the remaining 1-in (2.5-cm) discs and crosses using the method described in step 3. Suspend the 1-in (2.5-cm) discs, crosses and stones from the main bracelet, using irregular length chains made from pairs of jump rings to achieve a random effect.

It has taken a long time for plastics to shake off their unwarranted reputation as tawdry and disposable materials. In fact, the techniques involved in making this type of jewellery are often as complicated and skilled as those used in precious stonework or metalwork. With the development of the plastic craft maker, plastics are often convincing imitations of such natural materials as metal and glass. And those that are not can be equally attractive and comprise the bulk of the costume jewellery market.

Despite their contemporary connotations, plastics have a long history. Amber, horn, tortoiseshell and shellac are all natural plastics which were used for

century. In 1839 Charles Goodyear mixed latex and natural rubber with sulphur to produce a strong moulding rubber. The addition of more sulphur resulted in a hard, shiny material resembling jet, which became known as vulcanite or ebonite. Parkesine resembled ivory or horn and celluloid (cellulose nitrate), which became popular in jewellery-making in 1920, has a tortoiseshell appearance. The first true synthetics appeared in 1907 when the Belgian chemist Leo Baekeland produced phenolic resin. Even today, Bakelite is a familiar term, and this new heat-resistant resin was typically made in mottled effects of black, dark brown, green or red.

plastics

adornment, particularly in the 18th century. Horn is well suited to laminating techniques and the appeal of tortoiseshell comes from its striking natural markings. Amber is a hard, thermoplastic resin fossilized from primitive tree species and was used by the Greeks and Romans for shaping into jewellery.

Although today resins come in many different forms to suit different moulding processes, traditionally resin was tapped from trees. After straining, it was exposed to oxygen which caused the resin to harden in a process known as polymerization or curing.

Synthetics and semi-synthetics

Semi-synthetics – combinations of natural substances and certain catalysts – were developed in the 19th

The 1960s witnessed a plastics boom, particularly in acrylics and PVC. Following a quiet period during the 1970s, the punk era boosted plastics' profile once more, and the 1980s saw new and imaginative ways of creating plastic jewellery.

Basically, plastics can be used in two ways. First, they can be laser-cut from solid sheets for mass-production, or hand-sawn for one-offs (see Louise Slater's pieces overleaf). Alternatively, the material can be melted down, poured into a mould or hand-shaped, and then rehardened. Lil Gardner prefers to use the second method for her jewellery – she melts the plastic down into liquid form and then re-shapes it in a hand-made metal mould.

Previous page left to right: Bracelet of threaded plastic egg-shaped beads (Janet van der Pol); cast acrylic curved painted bangle (Rowena Park); red and pink button earring (Louise Slater); red bobble earrings and charm bracelet with candy-twist beads (Laura Lee); tear-drop surfboard-resin bead necklace (Dinosaur Designs); purple and red acrylic earring (Wilson Tontine);

Resins

Working with resins can be complicated because of the chemical hardening and accelerating processes necessary for the substance to "go off". There are two main categories of resin: polyester and epoxy. Polyester resin is a syrupy liquid, which becomes solid when a catalyst is added. Polyester resins should be stored in a cool, dark place and will last for 6-12 months. The catalyst requires the same environment, but should be used within three months.

More expensive epoxy resin is a clear substance which is suitable for casting, embedding and enamelling projects. Jenifer Corker uses an epoxy resin for her

Dinosaur Designs (see p.102), who fashion their beads in unique multi-moulds – this method enables them to produce lots of similar beads at the same time. In most instances, you take a mould from an original of the design, usually in wax. When working with plastic moulds, such as silicone rubber, acrylics and vinyls, a releasing agent is not normally necessary, but in some cases, however, when pouring silicone over a silicone mould, for example, it is needed. An easy releasing agent to make comprises five percent petroleum jelly in white spirit (mineral spirits).

Moulds can be made in either one or two pieces. For a one-piece mould, the original should be placed in a

&resins

pink and red bauble earring (Laura Lee); moulded resin bangle embedded with crushed and dyed free-range eggshell (Jenifer Corker); bracelet of multi-coloured linked discs (Lil Gardner); spandex cuff bracelet wired with assorted plastic beads and trinkets (Lil Gardner); gold and purple dangle earrings (Janet van der Pol); blue acrylic brooch (Louise Slater).

jewellery. She creates an original effect by mixing crushed eggshell or glitter with the clear liquid resin, before leaving it to set in a mould. Jenifer often casts the resin mixture in a solid silver mould which gives her pieces a "precious feel".

When creating resin jewellery the selection of the right mould is essential. Popular moulds include plaster of Paris, wood, polyester resin, latex, vinyl-based materials and silicone rubber. The silicone variety is ideal for all polyester resins, acrylics and low-melting metals. Silicone is a free-flowing rubber which should be mixed with a catalyst before use.

There are many imaginative ways for making moulds as proved by the Australian jewellery company,

box or frame and the catalyzed rubber poured slowly into the corner of the box until it completely surrounds the mould. Take care to avoid air bubbles – these can be removed by teasing them gently with a cocktail (swizzle) stick. The liquid is then left to cure or harden in the mould for about one hour. For a two-piece mould, embed half of the mould with white modelling clay, leaving the other half exposed. Fill the empty half with the catalyzed rubber mixture. Leave this to cure for about an hour, then remove the modelling clay and fill the second, empty half in the same manner.

Before pouring the resin into a mould, you need to measure the right amount of catalyst (hardener). The ratio of catalyst to resin should ideally comprise of one percent catalyst to 99 percent resin. Too much catalyst can result in an explosion. Most resins are pre-accelerated, but for those that are not it is important that you don't add the accelerator and catalyst simultaneously. Once the catalyst has been added, the polymerization, or curing, process commences, during which the resin becomes a liquid and then a gel before finally hardening. After this the resin requires a curing period. Unfortunately, there are no hard and fast rules governing this time, and most designers admit that they have arrived at their personal timings through trial and error. Factors that can affect curing time include draughts and dampness, which should be avoided, room temperature, the resin-moulding process used and the amount of resin involved. The recommended temperature for curing is 68°F (20°C). If you are working below this temperature, you should use additional accelerator.

Fillers and strengtheners

Fillers are normally used to improve colour, to produce metallic effects or to strengthen the resin and make it scratch-resistant. Fillers start off dry and are mixed in with the resin before the addition of the catalyst. Inert filler is specifically for use with polyester resin, making it durable and water-resistant. Metal fillers are used with cold-cast resin. These come in powdered form and comprise such metals as aluminium, copper, nickel or brass. Mineral Black darkens a bronze filler. Powdered pigments can also be used to colour resin. These can be either opaque or translucent. You can use more than one colour at a time, but it is important that you keep the mixture smooth.

Embedding

With the development of cold-setting resins in 1947, it became possible to embed insects, flowers and other natural objects into resin. The idea of embedding has since expanded and once the process has been mastered, it is possible to embed practically anything – size allowing.

The resin suitable for embedding is a water-clear polyester resin, which is pre-accelerated. The mould used should be half-filled with resin and three percent catalyst (instead of the normal one per cent). When this is firm, the leaf, insect, dried flower or whatever you are embedding should be positioned and covered with sufficient embedding resin to fill the mould. Polishing involves rubbing with wet-and-dry coarse sandpaper and gradually working down to a finer grade. To finish off, use a soft, lint-free cloth and metal polish to achieve a smooth glass-like finish. (Embedding is dealt with in more detail on p.100.)

Safety precautions

It is important that you follow strict safety rules when working with resin. Guidelines are available from all resin suppliers and manufacturers.

Make sure that you always use all resins and solutions in a well-ventilated room. Do not smoke or use accelerators directly with catalysts as this may result in an explosion. Resins should not come into contact with alkalis, fluorescent light fittings, flames, oxidizing agents or strong acids.

The fumes given off by resins are toxic and can cause nausea or dizziness, so always wear a mask when working with them. Wear protective clothing and avoid getting resin on your skin – either wear gloves or apply a barrier cream to your hands.

Before disposing of materials and chemical substances, check the relevant regulations with an environmental safety officer, as some local councils have strict rules regarding the disposal and incineration of chemical substances.

Provided that these precautions are taken seriously by the home-jeweller, there should be no cause for concern. Plastics and resins offer infinite new possibilities to the jewellery maker and, provided you have a suitable workspace and follow the instructions that are set out by the manufacturers carefully, they are easy to use at home.

Above: Laminates are available in a spectrum of different colours. This geometric-shaped brooch has been cut from pieces of pre-coloured laminate. Individual shapes are bevelled around the edges, scored to produce a contrasting design and then screwed together with pins. (Louise Slater)

Right: A striking collection of soft, organic shapes which have all been cut from plastic laminate and acrylic sheet. After chemically dyeing the individual pieces in a spectrum of vibrant, Mediterranean colours they are machine-polished to achieve a smooth surface. (Louise Slater)

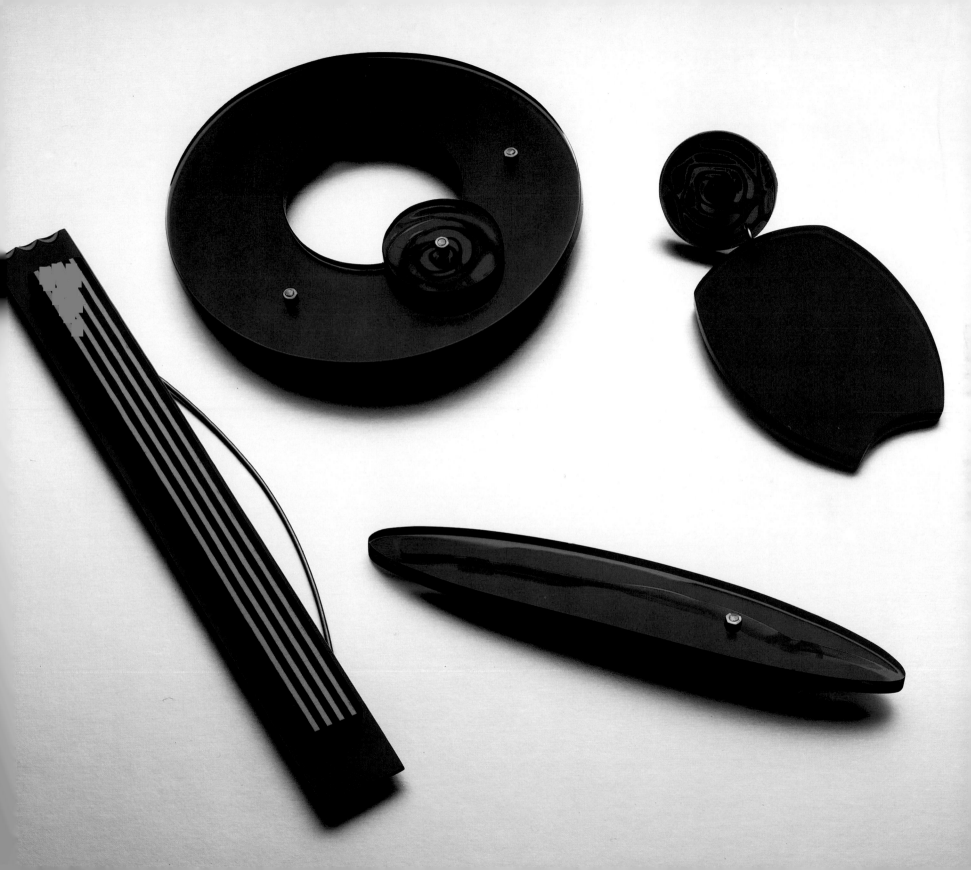

how to use **e**mbedding **r**esins

Equipment and materials

Embedding resin

Hardener

Releasing agent
(petroleum jelly)

2 leaves

Modelling clay

Mixing beaker

Swizzle (cocktail) stick

Fine wet-and-dry
sandpaper

Lint-free cloth

Metal polish

Drill

2 earclip findings

Knife

Wooden plug or piece
of tubing

Embedding resin is a water-clear polyester material, the special properties of which enable you to pour it into moulds as a clear thermo-setting liquid. Usually, it is used to sandwich an object – an autumn leaf in this instance – between two even layers to construct a piece of jewellery.

Many things can be embedded in resin; consider natural objects such as flowers, leaves and bark or man-made items like stamps, marbles, broken mirrors or coins. Seaweed is another unlikely but very effective basis for jewellery, as proved by Barbara Bosha Nelson who captures the wet-look of seaweed by preserving it in resin (see p.125). You can also set small, unusually shaped shells in resin as the foundation for easy-to-wear, lightweight pieces.

There are no hard and fast rules for embedding. Each embedding job will require a different amount of resin and catalyst (hardener) depending on the size of the object. Small quantities of resin are available from specialist resin supply firms (see p.140) for projects such as pieces of jewellery. The basic kit consists of liquid resin, hardener and moulds and is accompanied by a

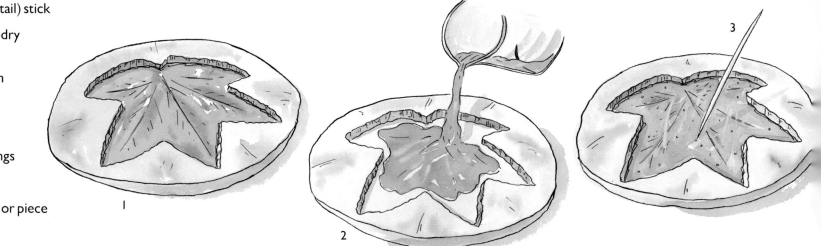

1 *Roll out a base platform of modelling clay about ¼in (5mm) thick or, ideally, use some form of flat surface smeared with a releasing agent. Then construct a modelling clay wall measuring about ½in (1.5cm) in height around the silhouette of the leaf shape. Build it as near as possible to the leaf without encroaching on it. Make sure that the inside of the mould is extremely smooth and leak-proof.*

2 *In a mixing beaker, make up a small quantity of resin according to the manufacturer's instructions, add the corresponding number of drops of hardener and stir gently with a* swizzle (cocktail) stick to avoid air bubbles. Carefully pour the resin into the mould. The resin will form the supporting layer for the leaf and should be sufficient just to cover the bottom of the mould (about 2mm deep).

3 *When the bottom layer has set, the exposed upper surface will remain tacky and this will help you to secure the leaf when you place it gently on top. Make up a second mixture of resin and hardener as before and pour it over the leaf, making sure that it is completely covered. Tease out any air bubbles by probing them with a cocktail (swizzle) stick or similar. Make*

comprehensive guide to the proportions of resin to use and the amount of catalyst or hardener you will require for each project. You do not have to use the moulds supplied – in the example featured here, because of the nature of the item being encapsulated, a mould was produced freehand from modelling clay.

Resin is a toxic substance, so make sure that you follow the safety precautions (set out on p. 98). Always work in a well-ventilated room and avoid getting resin on your skin (either apply a barrier cream to your hands or wear protective gloves).

Right: The beauty of working with resins is that you can permanently preserve an ephemeral, natural object – like this autumn leaf – in a clear solution. Once encapsulated, the object will retain its natural colour and form. The earclip finding was hand-painted with a cold-setting transparent resin – the colour has been chosen to complement and enhance the natural colours of the leaf. The brass earring findings are flanked by two berry-like beads. These have been chosen because their colour and form harmonize with the organic, autumnal theme.
(Barbara Bosha Nelson)

sure that the exposed mould is dust-proof by covering it gently with a piece of lint-free cloth.
4 *When the resin is completely cured (about 24 hours), remove the hardened block from the modelling clay. Remnants of clay wall will adhere to the edge of the resin, but you can remove this by scraping it away with a knife. The enclosed leaf will still retain surface tackiness; remove this by sanding with fine wet-and-dry sandpaper. Finally, to achieve a smooth, glass-like finish, buff carefully with metal polish and a completely lint-free cloth.*

5 *To make a hole to attach the finding, drill a hole at the top of the finished leaf with extreme care. Alternatively, you can make provisions to form a hole during the initial gel setting stage of the resin. The best way to do this is by inserting either a wooden plug or a small piece of tubing covered in releasing agent near the top of the embedded object just after the resin has been poured into the mould. Once the resin has set, pull or drill out the plug or tubing. You can decorate the front of the finding, as here, with a button or stone, attached with an appropriate glue (see p. 25).*

how to cut and form **c**ast **a**crylic

Equipment and materials

Workbench

Coloured cast acrylic
(Perspex) sheet (3mm
thick)

Thick cardboard to
form a template

Pencil or pen

Craft knife

Tape measure

Scorer or scalpel

Electric band saw

Safety mask

Safety goggles

Ear muffs

Coarse metal file

Wet-and-dry
sandpaper

Fine-grade sandpaper

Disc sander

Buff stick (optional)

Baking tray lined with a
protective layer of foil

Oven gloves

Wrist-sized tube or
glass jar/bottle

Plastic is a popular material for jewellery-making because it is light, strong, colourful and pliable. These characteristics make it an ideal material for producing large, brightly coloured pieces of jewellery. Wilson Tontine used Perspex by ICI for this bracelet, although there are other makes on the market. Perspex is manufactured in sheet form in 2-mm, 3-mm and 4-mm thicknesses and is available in clear, coloured, opaque or transparent finishes.

Whether you choose Perspex or another brand, make sure that you buy cast acrylic as this type of plastic can be heated in a domestic oven and then moulded into shape. The advantage of using cast acrylic for this bangle is that it is flexible and will withstand frequent bending – you can therefore practise the heating and knotting processes over and over again until you have achieved a satisfactory result. Cast acrylic will harden and set very quickly once it is removed from the oven, so at each attempt you will only have a few minutes to mould the bracelet into shape.

You can buy cast acrylic from signmakers or from specialist shops (see p.140). It is possible to dye cast

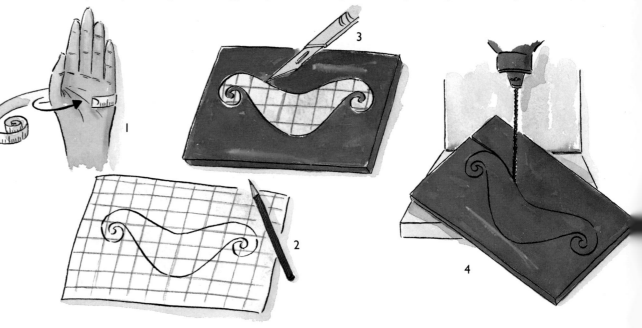

1 *To gauge the size of your bracelet, take a tape measure and wind it around your hand. Your hand will have to pass through the bracelet, so measure the circumference of your palm, starting at the joint at the base of your thumb – 8ins (20cm) approximately.*

2 *Decide on a shape and width for your bracelet. Draw this design to the exact proportions onto cardboard. (The main straight length will be equal to your hand's measurement, but you must allow for the curled ends which are knotted together.)*

3 *Cut out the shape with a craft knife. This cardboard pattern will be used as a template when you come to cut out the cast acrylic sheet.*

4 *Place the template on top of the coloured cast acrylic sheet and then score around the design using either a scalpel or scorer. Working at a workbench and wearing protective safety goggles, mask and earmuffs, carefully cut around this shape with a band saw.*

5 *Smooth the rough edges of the cast acrylic with a coarse*

acrylic yourself using textile dye, but since the material is available in such a wide range of colours you will find that it is easier to buy it ready-dyed.

An electric band saw is the ideal tool for cutting cast acrylic as long as you wear protective goggles, mask and earmuffs. Alternatively, you could use a piercing saw with a size 1 blade and offset teeth. Buy a coarse, rather than a fine, metal file for smoothing down the rough edges of the cast acrylic as it is less likely to clog. You can remove any file marks from cast acrylic by rubbing the surface vigorously with a buff stick.

Previous pages: Crafted from surfboard resin, this bold jewellery was inspired by rocks and seashells. Each silhouette is formed in a multi-mould, which allows for the creation of similar pieces at once, and then coloured in vibrant and translucent shades.
(Dinosaur Designs)

Right: Brightly coloured shaped acrylic pieces like this knotted bracelet are reminiscent of the Op-Art jewellery movement of the 1960s (see p.17). Available in a spectrum of colours, cast acrylic is easy to work with and can be heat-moulded into shape.
(Wilson Tontine)

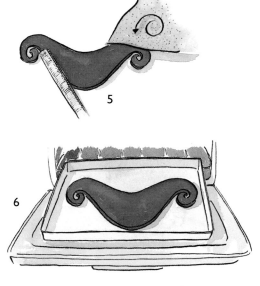

5

6

7

metal file, then sand both sides with wet-and-dry sandpaper. Use the disc-sander to bevel the edges and finish with finest grade sandpaper. You could also use a buff stick to smooth the edges; this will remove any file marks.

6 *Put the cast acrylic shape on a baking tray, lined with a protective layer of kitchen foil. Next heat the shape in a medium-hot oven for about one minute or until the acrylic is soft and malleable.*

7 *Remove the tray from the oven with oven gloves and, still*

wearing the gloves, immediately wrap the cast acrylic shape around a wrist-sized tube or jar. At the same time, knot the ends of the cast acrylic together and twist each end into a spiral pattern – the acrylic will not break but will harden and go brittle after a few minutes. Hold the moulded bracelet in place with gloved hands until it is completely set. If you are dissatisfied with the final shape of the bangle, you can return it to the oven where it will soften and revert to its original shape. Once it is soft, you can begin the knotting process again.

Enamel is a form of glass and enamelling is the process of fusing it to metal with heat. The earliest known example of enamelled jewellery is a set of Mycenaean beads which date back to 1450BC. Constructed using the *champlevé* method, they are made from blue enamel fused to decorative gold beads. During the 3rd and 2nd centuries BC, the Greeks employed a dipped enamelling technique which involved heating a piece of metal, immersing it in molten glass and then shaping it into jewellery. The Romans also used *champlevé* enamelling to decorate bronze medallions and brooches.

Byzantine enamel work, which was highly ornate and characterized by its use of bright, pure colours, had a great influence on the jewellery of the 5th and 10th

Battersea enamelled ware – white enamelled copper plaques decorated in coloured *grisaille* with portrait or flower motifs.

Most Art Nouveau enamel jewellery emanates from France with René Lalique as its finest creator. The jewellery of this period is characterized by its use of flowing lines, swirling curves, dragonflies, nude females and creeping vines. These motifs were displayed on brooches, pendants and necklaces and drew on the vivid colours used in Japanese enamel.

Using enamels

There are three types of enamel – opaque, transparent and opalescent. You can either buy enamel in lump form or as ready-ground grains. Enamel will last for tens

enamel

centuries. At this time, *cloisonné* enamelling was widely used. This technique superseded the relatively crude *champlevé* method and allowed for greater intricacy on much smaller pieces. Earrings depicting a bird design were typical of the period, as were medallion pendants and bracelets decorated with enamel.

During the 12th and 13th century, Limoges became the principle centre for the enamelling industry. During the 14th century, further refinements to techniques appeared, with *email en ronde bosse* or encrusted enamelling. This process of layering enamel in high relief was widely used during the Renaissance by artist craftsmen such as Hans Holbein the Younger who made jewellery for Henry VIII. The 18th century brought

of years in its lump form and can be ground as required – the ideal consistency is of granulated sugar. To obtain the correct consistency you must first grind the grains underwater with a pestle and mortar for about one minute – this process also purifies the enamel and removes any contaminating particles. Carefully pour off the cloudy water and repeat the rinsing process until the water runs clear and you achieve grains of an equal size – this may take 10-12 rinses. Put the ground enamel into a clean ceramic saucer, cover it with a piece of paper and dry it under a lamp or beside a kiln. Store the dried granules in an airtight container out of direct sunlight.

Preparation

The first step for all enamelling techniques is to clean

the metal base (enamel will not adhere to an oxidized or greasy surface). First, anneal the metal (see p.84), then cool it and immerse it in cold water. Put it into a pickling solution (see p.85) of 8½fl.oz (250ml) vinegar to one dessertspoon of salt for 10 minutes. Remove the clean metal with tweezers and rinse it under running water – do not touch the clean metal with your fingers as you may deposit grease on the surface.

Enamel application

There are two methods for applying enamel to metal – dusting (which is unsuitable for small items of jewellery) and wet-laying. For wet-laying, put a little enamel powder into a clean ceramic dish and mix it with distilled water by degree. Apply the resulting mixture thinly and evenly over small areas of the metal base with a quill or brush. If the enamel forms lumps and drops off, it is too wet; if it sticks to the quill, it is too dry. Tap the enamelled disc to remove air bubbles, soak up any excess moisture with a paper towel and place it near a kiln until it has thoroughly dried out.

Firing

Although you can use a blow torch for enamelling (see p.112), to achieve good results, it is advisable that you use a kiln. Small, purpose-built kilns are available from craft stores. Since the temperature necessary for firing enamel is very high – 1652°F (900°C) – make sure that you supervize children at all times.

Before you enamel the top side of your metal disc, you must first counter-enamel the reverse side. This process is designed to prevent the flat metal shape from warping and curving as it cools. The counter enamel layer counteracts the tensions that result from the firing and cooling processes and prevents the enamel's surface from cracking. Wet-lay the reverse side of your clean, metal surface and, using tweezers, put the enamel-coated disc onto a panning mesh. Using a firing fork, put it into the kiln (this should be pre-heated at 1652°F (900°C)). After about 30 seconds, open the kiln door and quickly check the enamel. When it becomes

bright, smooth and glossy, remove it from the the kiln and cool, then clean the base with steel wire and a solution of vinegar and salt. The top side is now ready for wet-laying and firing. Apply the moist enamel to the top side and, using tweezers, place it onto a panning mesh supported by a stilt to prevent the base from sticking to the wire mesh. Heat the disc in the kiln using the same method as described above.

There are many other methods for enamelling, but most of these are complicated and require specialist equipment and materials. For example, *champlevé* enamelling involves carving out a design in the metal's surface and wet-laying moist enamel into the depressions. *Cloisonné* enamelling is a method of enclosing coloured enamel in small, wire compartments or cells. The *cloisonné* wire, which is made from either copper, gold or silver, is cut and shaped with pliers and is then applied to a metal base using clear enamel in your chosen design. After firing in a kiln, the compartments are wet-laid with thin and even layers of clear enamel. *Plique à jour* enamelling is a similar technique to *cloisonné* in so far as the enamel is enclosed in wire cells, but for this method, there is no metal backing behind the enamel, so the translucent colours take on the appearance of a stained-glass window.

Two other well-known enamelling techniques are *Limoges* (painted enamel) and *grisaille* (monochrome painting). For the *Limoges* method, enamel the metal base with three thin layers of white enamel. After firing in a kiln, draw a design onto the surface enamel and dry under a lamp (the heat of a kiln is such that it will distort the colours). In the *grisaille* process, the surface of the metal base is enamelled with three thin layers of black enamel which are then fired before layering the surface with white *grisaille* enamel mixed with the painting medium. The result is a gray enamel ground which is then built up with layers of black, gray, brown or purple enamel of differing thicknesses, creating a subtle relief effect.

Above: This pewter brooch is cold-enamelled. As its name suggests, this method does not require the use of a kiln and is therefore much easier to carry out than traditional enamelling. You can buy cold enamelling kits, complete with instructions, from craft suppliers (see p.140). (Jane Crawford)

Right: Decorated with the *cloisonné* technique, this collection of enamelled, silver brooches was inspired by the sea. First, the silver is hand-forged and acid-etched. Next, the coloured enamelled decoration is applied in layers and then the piece is fired in a kiln. (Julia Cook)

how to **e**namel

Equipment and materials

Powder enamel in
assorted colours

Blow torch

3 fire bricks

Fine-mesh steel trivet

Copper disc or small
amount of copper
sheeting (at least
0.5mm thick)

Steel wool or emery
paper

Painter's palette

Paint brush

Spatula

2 earring findings

4 cuttle-fish bones

Iron binding wire

Sharp, fine-pointed
tool (eg. scalpel)

Wire cutters

Fine-grade sandpaper

Pewter

Steel ladle with a lip
around its edge

Oven gloves

Glue or solder to
attach earring findings

Enamel is painted onto a copper base and fired in a kiln to produce a hard finish. It is available in bright or pastel colours and in matte, shiny, opaque and transparent finishes. To make up enamel paste, scoop a little powdered enamel onto a painter's palette or saucer. Add a very small amount of distilled water by degree and combine the ingredients with a spatula until the mixture forms a paste. Cover with a sheet of paper to prevent contamination from dust particles.

Before you begin enamelling, you must first roughen the surface of your copper base shape by rubbing it with steel wool or fine-grade emery paper, because the enamel paste will not adhere to a smooth surface. When it is placed in a kiln or heated with a blow torch, the enamel will melt and fuse with the metal. Although it is possible to buy copper shapes from a specialist craft

1 *Using a paint brush, apply a little enamel paste over the roughened surface of the copper shape. Leave the enamel-coated shape in a warm place until the water evaporates and the enamel sets. (It is important that all the moisture evaporates, otherwise the enamel will crack and lift off while it is being heated.) Once the enamel is completely dry, put the copper shape onto a fine-mesh trivet supported by fire bricks.*

2 *Apply a gentle heat from the lighted blow torch to the underside of the copper (not the enamel-coated side). Heat the shape gradually, making sure that you use a soft flame. Do not apply heat directly onto the enamel surface. After about a minute, the enamel should start to melt. Once the enamel begins to form a glass-like surface, switch off the blow torch and leave*

the shape to cool for 10-15 minutes. If you want to create a pattern using a contrasting colour, allow the first enamel layer to cool, then paint a different-coloured enamel over the first coat, to a design – dots, for example – that leaves some of the first layer of colour exposed. Heat and cool the second layer using the same methods as for the first enamel layer.

3 *Make up the mould for the pewter from cuttle-fish bones. Level off the soft side of the two cuttle-fish bones by rubbing them vigorously with sandpaper. Next, carve your desired shape into the middle of the levelled-off soft side with a scalpel. (Make sure that you carve a shape with a recess of a suitable depth and size to take the enamelled shape at the next stage.) When you are satisfied with the design, use the scalpel to carve out a v-shaped*

shop, you may prefer to make one up to your own specifications. If you decide to make your own copper shape, draw your design onto a piece of copper with a scriber, clamp the copper into a jeweller's peg and cut it out carefully using a piercing saw (see p.92).

You can buy pewter from specialist stores (see p.140), while cuttle-fish bones are available from pet food stores or you may find them washed up on the beach.

(see p.92)
(see p.140)

Right: These sunburst earrings, based on natural organic shapes, are cast in molten pewter. This is poured into a carved cuttle-fish bone mould where it is left to set. The cuttle-fish bone's rough surface gives the cast pewter an uneven, textured finish. The central painted shape is made from enamel paste which, when heated, fuses with its copper base to form a glass-like surface. (Louise Nagle)

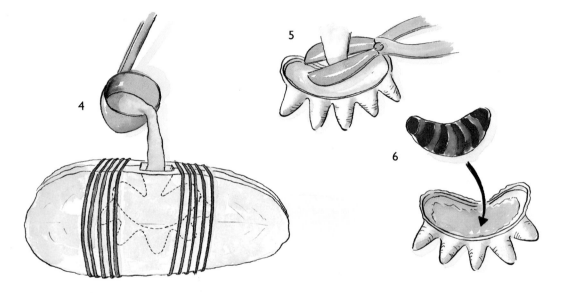

channel leading from the outer rim of the bone to the carved design (the pewter will be poured through this channel into the carved mould). The second cuttle-fish bone will form the reverse side of the mould and must be left plain. Keeping the levelled-off sides together, bind the cuttle-fish bones together extremely tightly using iron binding wire. Support the cuttle-fish mould between two fire bricks, making sure that the channel opening is pointing upward.

4 *Pour enough pewter to fill the mould into a steel ladle supported by fire bricks or a heat-resistant platform. Wearing oven gloves, support the handle of the ladle with your hand and apply heat from the blow torch to the underside of the ladle. After about 10 minutes, the pewter will become molten.*

Keeping the ladle under sustained heat from underneath, carry the ladle toward the mould (do not allow the pewter to cool at this stage). Pour the molten pewter into the mould through the channel opening. Once the pewter fills to the top of the v-shaped channel, leave the mould to cool for about 10 minutes.

5 *Unbind the wire wrapped around the two cuttle-fish bones and separate them. Snip away the v-shaped pewter channel with wire cutters and discard. Tidy up your pewter shape by filing away any rough edges with sandpaper.*

6 *Finally, glue the enamelled shape into its central recess, turn it over and glue or solder an earring finding to the back (see p.42 for soldering instructions). When you make up the second earring make sure that you use a new cuttle-fish bone mould.*

(see p.42 for soldering instructions)

From ancient times, gemstones have been synonymous with folklore and legend since every stone is believed to have its own magical property. Even today, stones are still worn as amulets in India to fend off disease. Stones were traditionally divided into two categories – precious and semi-precious – but today both groups come under the generic name, gemstone.

Precious stones are diamonds, rubies, sapphires and emeralds, while the semi-precious group includes amber, jasper, quartz, agate, amethyst, jade, jet, lapis lazuli, turquoise, aquamarine, opal and zircon. Some stones, for example jasper and quartz, were mined as long ago as 300,000-12,000BC, while sapphires, diamonds and rubies were not mined until about 500BC.

While semi-precious and precious stones are mined from rocks, organic stones are sourced in other ways. These are living entities and include pearl, coral, amber, jet and tortoiseshell. Pearls come from the pearl mussel and oyster and can't be synthesized although they can be cultured – a process that takes a few years. Coral is a polyp of jelly attached to rocks, while amber, which originated in prehistoric times, is a sticky resin that comes from coniferous trees. Jet, a popular jewellery material during Victorian times, is derived from fossilized wood which has been subjected to stagnant water and pressure. Fossils and pebbles can also be set and mounted as stones, as can petrified wood, which takes on a high lustre when it is polished.

Previous page left to right: Gilded ceramic necklace (Elizabeth Hainski); embossed silver and lapis lazuli ring (Annaliese); twisted silver and semi-precious stone necklace (Julia Cook); glass pebble and silver earrings (Bernard O'Reilly); mosaic glass earrings (Simon Rees and Susan Small); silver and slate bracelet (Carlo Giovanni Verda); silver and cabochon stone ring (Crowther & Sieff);

stones

Gemstones are frequently substituted with imitations, however stone copying is by no means a modern concept. The early Egyptians used quartz-coated coloured glass in place of gemstones, while the Romans used paste stones to imitate transparent and opaque gems. Paste stones were also used during the Italian Renaissance, at which time gem engraving and carving, an art which dates back to Babylonian times, was also prolific. In 1891, Auguste Verneuil, the pioneer of gem synthesis, originated a method to synthesize stones from alumina and powdered oxide. Today, the most important synthetic stones are Strontium Titanate, synthesized in 1955 to imitate diamond, and Yttrium Aluminium Garnet, which is more brilliant than diamond but not as hard.

Preparing stones

Most designers prefer to buy ready-faceted gemstones from a lapidary supplier (someone who cuts and engraves stones). Tumbling is a mechanical process designed to polish and round rough stones by duplicating the natural action whereby rocks fall and rub against each other. The process involves spinning the stone in a revolving barrel with water and abrasive and finally a polishing powder. In nature the process takes thousands of years, but it only takes a few hours in a tumbling machine and you can achieve a much higher gloss.

While transparent stones are best faceted, opaque stones also work well with cabochon cuts. Cutting *en cabochon* is relatively simple and involves using a trim saw to shape the stone into a dome shape on a flat base.

marble brooch set with silver spheres (Alison MacCulloch); gold-plated necklace with gemstones (Van der Straeten); Italian marble earrings (Alison MacCulloch); pebble brooch (Louise Slater); gemstone bracelet (Tom McEwen).

Opposite: These ceramic shapes are glazed with 22-carat gold or copper lustre to make them resemble highly polished metal. (Elizabeth Hainski)

Faceted stones, which are cut with many faces to catch the light, result in a more brilliant stone. Today, stone cutting is usually carried out with an electric cutting and slabbing machine. After cutting, stones are lapped – this involves splitting the stone with a series of revolving vertical wheels or laps, then grinding with horizontal laps – and finally polished and lubricated. If you decide to cut your own stones, make sure that you practise first on quartz or rock crystal before moving to more precious stones. Always follow the stone's natural cleavage – the direction of the plane along which it is most easily split.

Mounting and setting stones

Cut stones can either be partly drilled for mounting or fully drilled and strung onto cord or wire. For soft substances, such as amber and marble, you can use a hand or bench steel drill, while a solid metal drill with diamond grit is recommended for harder substances (this should be used in conjunction with a lubricant – either oil or water). To keep small stones and beads steady while you are hand-drilling them, simply cement them in hard shellac wax. First, heat the shellac wax to facilitate embedding, insert the stone and leave it to cool. Once cold, the wax will hold the stone fast. You can remove the stone by re-melting the shellac.

There are many different ways to set stones into a metal base. These include closed set, where the part of the stone below the girdle (the widest circumference) is embedded in metal, or open set where the base (pavilion) of the stone is also exposed to light except for where it is being supported (in this instance, the stone is usually secured with a set of upward projecting prongs).

The most popular ring setting is the claw setting where the stone's crown is held by a series of projecting prongs, while the cluster setting, where a group of stones surround the largest central stone, is also widely used. A *pavé* setting is a mass of small, closely fitting stones which completely conceal the metal. Channel settings are single rows of stones of the same size which bridge two metal bands. For a collet setting, the top of a metal band is bent over the stone to secure it. Because of the delicate nature of stones, make sure that you hold them with a pair of serrated tweezers with retractable jaws while mounting.

A setting is known as a collet and can either be a plain band or a series of prongs. The setting should include a bezel, a ledge on which the stone's girdle rests, which can be made by soldering a strip of narrow metal along the middle of a metal strip to make a ledge. This can then be shaped with pliers to fit the stone and the overlap sawn off. The two bezel ends are then soldered together. An alternative method is to carve a ledge into a thicker piece of metal with a bull stick.

Pearls require a different setting technique and the use of white pearl cement which, unlike adhesive, will not discolour. This can be melted if necessary to allow for easy removal of the pearl. Round pearls are set in a cup through which a piece of wire is soldered. The pearl is partially drilled and cemented onto the wire.

Coloured glass is a centuries-old substitute for stone. Coloured glass pieces were originally backed with foils in closed settings, resembling stone jewellery, and in 1724 George Stras invented Strass, a brilliant lead glass. Surprisingly, it is common practice to artificially colour semi-precious and precious stones to improve their original appearance and value. This is often carried out on rose quartz and amethyst which are prone to fading when exposed to strong sunlight.

The sheer beauty of stones is often enough to tempt a jeweller into working with them. Before you embark on stone-cutting and setting, make sure that you fully understand the subject of gemmology, which extends beyond the details covered in this chapter. When working with stones, their structure, colour and unique properties must be taken into consideration. Fortunately, for those who are not ambitious enough to carry out their own faceting, lapidaries will do most of the preparation work for you, after which the creation of eye-catching jewels is only limited by your imagination.

Above: A unique gold and silver ring, set with an oval amethyst stone hand-carved in a floral design. Unusual raised decoration adds interest to a plain, antiqued band – the silver twists and gold curled trimmings have been carefully soldered into place.
(Tom McEwen)

Right: This intricate, hand-tooled, solid silver suite of signet ring, star-shaped brooch, ornate bracelet and sceptral hat pin are set with red cornelian and green serpentine semi-precious stones. The silver must be hand-forged before it is twisted into place.
(Julia Cook)

how to **m**ount a **s**tone

Equipment and materials

6 cabochon stones

Blow torch

Steel tweezers

Steel textured hammer

Thin brass or copper sheeting

Piercing saw

Round-nosed pliers

Scriber

Fine metal file

Cardboard

Paper

Lead solder

Safety flux

Soldering iron

Paint brush

Pencil

Scissors

Charcoal block

Workbench with peg

Quick-setting glue

2 earclip findings

The three stones mounted on these earrings are all cabochon-style stones. This is the most suitable type of stone to use for this design as it has a flat back and, invariably, a domed top. A cabochon-style stone can be placed directly onto a flat metal surface and glued into place without the need for any setting.

There are a huge variety of solders on the market. If you choose to set the stones before you solder the settings to the main body of the earring, as in the instructions, make sure that you use a lead solder. If you prefer to use silver solder make sure that you set the stones at the final stage (after the five-point settings have been soldered into place.)

The amount of copper or brass sheeting you require will depend on the size of your stones. To estimate the quantity you will need for each stone, measure your

1 *To make the five-pointed star shape setting which will enclose the stone, put a cabochon stone onto a piece of thin cardboard and draw around the stone with a pencil. Draw five equal-sized triangular points protruding from this central oval shape. The length of each point, from its base to its tip, should measure about ⅓in (1cm). When you are satisfied with the shape of the cardboard star, cut it out carefully with a pair of scissors. Put this cardboard template onto the sheet metal. Draw around the star shape with a scriber and clamp the sheet metal into the bench peg. Using the piercing saw, carefully cut out the star shape.*

2 *Next, smooth down any rough edges with a fine metal file. Make a star shape for each stone using the same methods.*

3 *To create the rippled and beaten texture, each star setting must be annealed (see p.84). Hold the metal star with a pair of steel tweezers over a charcoal block or a strong surface that will withstand heat and hammer blows. Apply heat from the blow-torch to the entire surface of the star.*

4 *When it is red-hot, put the shape onto the steel block and hammer it vigorously with a steel hammer, observing the texture constantly. (The metal shape may need re-annealing as it will become hard and rigid and may crack if it is hammered when it is cold.)*

5 *Once you have achieved a satisfactory textured effect, leave the stars to cool. Once each shape is cold, carefully begin to bend the claws of each of the five star points upward with a pair of*

stone's diameter and treble that figure. (For example if your stone is ½in (1.3cm) in diameter, allow a piece of sheeting 1½in (4cm) square for each stone. Multiply this number by the number of stones you have decided to set – if you are setting six stones, buy a piece of metal 9in (24cm) square.) Gold plating metal is a complex procedure so I suggest that you send your earrings to a professional plater (see p.140) for finishing.

Right: A pair of textured gold-plated metal earrings that are embellished with semi-precious stones. The amethyst and moss-agate cabochon stones are held in place by claw settings. (Van der Straeten)

Overleaf: Natural found pebbles can be drilled and effectively mounted for jewellery – these have been bound onto plastic laminate and secured on the reverse with black nylon thread. (Louise Slater)

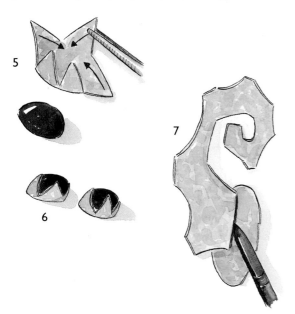

pliers, but make sure that you leave them sufficiently open to be able to slot the stone into the setting.

6 *Apply a drop of quick-setting glue to the middle of each setting and place the stone inside. Bend the claws of the setting upward and inward until they fit closely around the stone.*

7 *The main body of the earring is made up of a crescent shape with three protrusions and a leaf shape which is attached across the straight end and acts as a base onto which the earring clasp is soldered. Make a cardboard template of the crescent and leaf shapes and cut them out. Place the templates on the sheet metal and draw around them with a scriber. Cut out both shapes with a piercing saw and file away any rough edges.*

8 *Anneal both shapes, using the methods described in step 3.*

To solder the leaf shape to the flat end of the crescent shape, paint a little flux onto the middle of the leaf. Switch the soldering iron on. Unwind some solder and touch it with the tip of the iron – a small amount of solder should adhere to the iron (if it does not, allow more time for the iron to heat). Next, touch the flux-coated leaf shape with the tip of the iron – a little molten solder should adhere. Push the end of the crescent shape onto the leaf shape so that the leaf lies horizontally across the edge of the crescent shape. Leave to cool. Solder the cabochon stones in their settings onto the protruding tips of the crescent shape. Then solder the finding to the back of the leaf shape in the same way. If you are using silver solder, insert the stones in their settings at this stage.

Unorthodox materials are a limitless source of inspiration for making fascinating, seductive and unique jewellery. The widespread use of "found" objects in jewellery exemplifies how innovative contemporary designers have become in their location and utilization of materials around them; the boundaries of the imagination are stretched so far that practically any inanimate object has been used. Today's new breed of jewellers are like scavengers – not looking for their next meal, but for discarded junk and general flotsam and jetsam to inspire and feed their artistic appetites.

Found art is by no means a new medium. The concept of foraging and collecting elements to create beautiful things was in vogue long before many precious stones were discovered. By definition, primitive crafts-men were "found artists" using anything at hand – from teeth, bones and feathers to berries, flowers, shells and wood – to embellish themselves with.

Tongue-in-cheek found-art jewellery, which had its heyday in the 1930s, was inspired by surrealist art. Elsa Schiaparelli's "anything goes" designs were worn by everyone, from the Duchess of Windsor to Marlene Dietrich; they were both beautiful and wild and amusing. Her choice of materials included string, ostrich feathers and rubber and her homespun philosophy soon spread to the United States, where organic materials like walnuts, wood, acorns and cork were just some of the new jewellery components. Bette Davis soon became a fan of natural jewels – among her favourites were shells from Waikiki, lacquered coral and lime, iridescent pine cones and eucalyptus pods.

During the 1970s, more experimentation was carried out, inspired by mundane, environmental waste products. Swiss designer, Bernard Schobinger, based a whole series of jewellery pieces on the theme of the "throw-away society", using anything from shampoo sachets to pieces of park railing. In Britain, the idea expanded to shells, ring pulls, lacquered bones, pheasant feathers, juke box parts and even pasta. The use of functional, inexpensive and accessible items soon became a witty and fashionable art form.

While it is acceptable for designers to create theatrical, rather than realistic, pieces, some mould their jewellery to mirror their own socio-political ideals. Canadian jeweller, David Didur, produced a necklace in the shape of the United States, out of meshed matchsticks, firecrackers and electrical wire. He called the pendant "Medal for Dishonour" – a protest against the use of cruise missiles. Violent imagery was also a part of the revolutionary "punk" fashion movement of the late 1970s. Piercing safety pins, bicycle chains and even swastikas were worn as jewellery by the followers of the new punk "tribe".

The early 1980s saw the introduction of a cavalcade of dandified pop groups, which in turn inspired young but dedicated followers of fashion to emulate their heroes. A tidal wave of glitzy paste jewellery and accessories hit the fashion market. Progressive jewellery designers started to look in other directions for materials to use in place of the ubiquitous mass-produced paste and diamanté. Disregarding intrinsic monetary value, they flouted convention by concocting a visually stunning

found media

cocktail of sometimes quite mundane, sometimes bizarre, but always unexpected materials to create innovative jewellery.

Man-made ingredients

In 1983, Michael de Nardo first began disguising found objects by using and mixing together only small pieces, like the prong of a fork on the loop of a chain, so that their origins were not immediately obvious to the eye. He says that his intention is to elevate junk to the same level as quality jewellery. He combs flea markets for chain mail, old sixpences and "any simplistic piece I can manipulate into something else".

The majority of found artists prefer to leave their paraphernalia in its identifiable form and John Wind, who designed his first ragamuffin-style watch in 1986, is one of them. His non-functional debut piece was made up of four 1930s tank watches linked with brass and silver-plated links. He has now produced retro-style working watches in the same format and collage jewellery. His skills are varied: they range from embossing a Mona Lisa cameo with a fragmented rhinestone to preserving flowers in resin. As a result, his jewellery reworks and reinterprets, in a contemporary form, the delicacy of much Victorian jewellery.

Ieneke Boissevain's jewellery also has some historical value. She cannibalizes anything which originally had a religious, symbolic or decorative function, such as buttons, diamanté, charms, talismans, rosary beads and crucifixes, and transforms them into one-off "indulgent" pieces (see p.124). Although Ieneke trained as a jeweller, she "prefers to see what suggests itself".

At the other end of the spectrum, technology is a rich source of ideas. For example, computer or compact discs can be transformed into lightweight medallions, while Barbara Bosha Nelson creates unique earrings from black and white typewriter keys (see p.125).

Objects found in the home like elastic bands, paper clips, wires from glasses, keys, coins and broken china can all be incorporated into exciting and unusual pieces of jewellery – look at the work of Simon Milburn on p.124 for inspiration. Everyday objects can also inspire the shape of the piece – Ralph Turner's "Fancy Goods" collection incorporated miniature cans of baked beans, cereal packets and even hair-dryers. The Pop Art movement turned plastic into jewellery disguised as biscuits, fried eggs and chocolate.

Bottles, cut or uncut, are flexible "urban jewels". Uncut, they can be "heat-sagged" into various shapes, or simply used as a mould; irregularly sliced rims are good for free-form rings. It is recommended that you cut bottles and salvaged window glass with a bottle-cutter, using masking or drafting tape as a guide. Transparent glass lacquer paints dry quickly and are an ideal decoration for fragmented designs.

Peter Foster cuts sheets of industrial glass to produce large, sculptural pieces of jewellery, like his "foot long" brooches. He colours and etches the glass himself, rather than use pre-stained glass, and then ties the pieces together with silver wire. Sometimes he substitutes glass with copper and nickel "waste products".

Aluminium cans are another popular medium and their protective coatings respond well to fabric dye. Philippa Dutton collects old and new tins, already printed with floral designs, cuts them out with tin clips or shears and solders them together to produce brooches, earrings and hat pins in the form of bouquets. Tin is easy to solder and can also be combined with other materials such as brass. Because found media jewellery is, on the whole, not compatible with mass-production, all of her pieces are unique.

Like any junk enthusiast, urban jewellers see a scrap-metal yard as a magic kingdom. Cans, wheels and camping utensils can all be transformed with the use of a drill and a pair of pliers.

Simon Milburn bends and shapes nickel and silver-plated cutlery into unusual and figurative jewellery. He combines cutlery fragments such as the end of a fork with the curve of a spoon to produce pieces that bear

Above: A real ammonite fossil has been used to produce this dangle earring, which is embellished with snail-like twists of soldered silver wire and assorted semi-precious stones – even the earring finding has been concealed behind a coiled fossil shape.
(Donna Louise Iredale)

little resemblance to eating implements until you scrutinize them carefully.

Natural ingredients

Many natural sources can be located on the beach – a favourite haunt for some of the designers featured in this book. Cuttle-fish bones can be used successfully for pewter casting (see p.112), while beachcomed glass and pebbles can be drilled and mounted as pendants. Driftwood too, with its ingrained grooves and spirals, makes a good jewellery source. However, because of its porous nature, make sure that you seal it first with varnish or acrylic.

Katherine Wilkins' 4-inch (10-cm) box pendants (see p.132), designed to hold door keys and money, are perfect examples of "something precious" created from offcuts of wood. Their practical and unique design was based on Celtic relics. Katherine's range also includes burnt wood totem pole earrings complete with emblems. All of her pieces have been aged with paint-scrubbing techniques – they are designed to look as though "they've been underground for a century and a half".

Although she doesn't comb the coastline for them, fossils are a source of inspiration for Donna Louise Iredale, who transforms them into anything from buttons to bracelets. She cleans the fossils, cuts them on a grinding stone and then heats them to achieve a metallic finish. Donna then drills a hole into the middle and threads them onto wire, together with beads, silver, gold or semi-precious stones. Slate, which has a naturally rippled surface and metallic finish, is another of her favourite materials.

The seashore is also awash with feathers. The unpolluted kind can be mixed with fibres or metals to create an elaborate design. Feathers are widely used for ornamentation – in primitive cultures they were incorporated in traditional regalia such as head-dresses and their textural qualities are widely recognized by weavers. Feathers are available from farms and pet stores – more exotic ones are sometimes supplied by zoos.

Bones too, frequently occur in jewellery collections. Alice Shannon is internationally famous for her pieces which derived from bones and teeth. Her ornaments include turkey and chicken bones coated with black acrylic paint, cuttle-fish bones flanked with seal's teeth, and even the skull and jaw bones of a wild goose.

Woven grass and straw is used widely for jewellery-making across Africa. Large seeds are polished and pierced to make pendants and ostrich shell, bone, ivory, wood and horn are used to make beads. The Rudraksha nut is used for prayer beads by the Hindus. In the Pacific, tree fern and coconut palm are used for decorative hair combs, while head ornaments are made from the shells of giant clams and turtles.

Cultures worldwide have drawn inspiration from natural, locally found objects. Materials range from shells, porcupine quills, indigenous plants and snake-skin to the iridescent wings of beetles.

In this chapter I have examined how natural materials can be used to decorate the exterior of jewellery. However, found objects can also be used as a foundation for jewellery-making – gourds, melons, squash and any other firm vegetables make ideal cores for ceramic, papier mâché or clay items.

Natural media can also be used as "tools" or patterns to decorate jewellery. For instance, prints can be taken from leaves or even fish skin in the same way as a brass rubbing, but using waterproof inks, mixed with glycerine, and rice paper rather than crayons. Or foods such as popcorn, allspice and mustard seeds can be used for mosaic-style decoration (make sure that you heat the seeds first to prevent them from germinating).

What the use of found media in jewellery has proved is that people are willing to spend money on pieces that, although they have no financial value, are desirable for their creative ingenuity. Miscellanies of all shapes, sizes and forms surround us, and searching for them will awaken you to the limitless resources that are available for creative jewellery-making.

Above: Many unorthodox materials can be used for contemporary jewellery design, like this prehistoric-looking, hand-made concrete pebble. This is shaped with a central hole and attached to a hand-made oxidized-wire earring finding.
(Katherine Wilkins)

how to make a **w**ooden **p**endant

Equipment and materials

Thin offcuts of wood
¼in (7mm) thick to
include: 2 squares
2¼in² (5.8cm²)
2 quadrangles 2¼in x
3½in x 2in x 3½in
(5.8cm x 9cm x 5cm x
9cm)

Assorted found
objects

3ft (1.5m) rope or
cord

1½-2ft (45-60cm) thin
copper wire

Small tacks or nails

Wood glue

Medium-grade
sandpaper

Fine-grade sandpaper

Drill

G-clamps

Woodstain (optional)

Soft brush (optional)

Katherine Wilkins' box pendants are as practical as they are unique. She draws her inspiration from Celtic relics and emphasizes the antique and worn appearance of the boxes by applying a thin coat of white paint to the surface of the wood which she then scrubs off with coarse-grade sandpaper.

If you prefer a darker finish, you could apply a wood stain to the box with a soft cloth or paint brush or you could scorch the surface with a hot poker. For a textured pattern, try engraving a rough design into the surface of the wood with a narrow chisel or a sharp object.

(Decorative wood finishes are described in more detail on p.54.)

You can embellish your stained box with any found objects you choose (see p.124 for ideas). These may include drilled coins, pieces of broken jewellery or beachcombed glass or trinkets that you have salvaged from flea markets or junk stores. You can bind these small metal or glass pieces to the finished box using household electrical wire (available in gold, red and silver colours from hardware stores), and small tacks or nails or simply secure them with a strong cement-based glue.

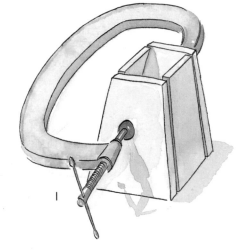

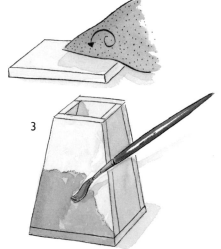

1 *To assemble your shapes of wood, apply a good-quality wood adhesive to the longest side edges of the four quadrangular box pieces. Clamp the sides together using G-clamps and allow the adhesive to dry for the allotted time (drying times will vary depending on the manufacturer).*

2 *Once the piece is dry, remove the clamps. Apply the wood adhesive around the perimeter of the box's base and place the box on top of the square piece of wood you have allocated for the base. Secure with G-clamps and leave to dry.*

3 *When the box is thoroughly dry, remove the G-clamps and* vigorously sand the entire box (including the lid) with coarse-grade sandpaper (either sand manually or use an electric sander for speed). This process should eliminate all rough edges and sharp corners. Next, sand with fine-grade sandpaper until you have achieved a smooth surface finish.

If you wish to colour the box, apply a wood stain using a soft brush or a paint brush and leave it to dry. If you want to achieve a darker finish, apply a second coat of stain. (Experiment with surface finishes beforehand on a spare offcut of wood as different woods react to stains in different ways.)

Katherine Wilkins uses pieces of found driftwood or any thin wood for her pendants, which she cuts to size by hand. However, you could acquire offcuts of wood from a local wood-merchant.

Although the pendant in the illustration is constructed using irregular quadrangular shapes of wood with uneven-length sides, you may find it easier to use four rectangular pieces of wood for the sides of your pendant – these are easier to measure and cut into shape and can be assembled in the same way as the quadrangular shapes that are illustrated in the diagram.

Previous pages: Natural horn is drilled, sanded, polished and then threaded, together with natural stones and horn beads, onto suede thonging to create organic-looking jewellery. The long necklace on the right is made from stained, polished and drilled almond stones. (Eric Beamon)

Right: Both functional and decorative, this laced box necklace is designed to hold small objects like lipsticks and keys. The sides of the box are embellished with aged shrapnel-like pieces of metal which enhance the antiqued look of the finished piece. (Katherine Wilkins)

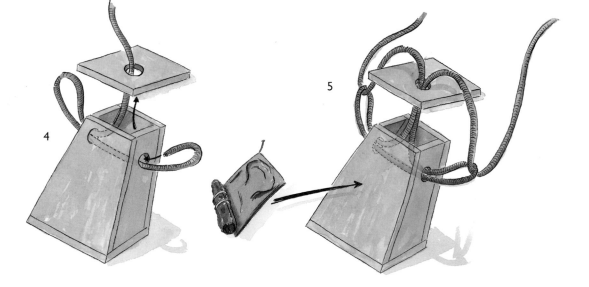

Once you are satisfied with the colour, leave the box to dry for the allotted time. See p.54 for further instructions and ideas for staining and finishing wood.

To make the holes for the cord, mark a halfway point 1½in (4cm) from the top edge of two of the narrowest sides of the box. To attach the lid, mark a point ½in (1.5cm) from the edge of the two opposite sides of the lid. Using an electric- or hand-drill, carefully drill out the marked holes in the lid and box, making sure that the holes are large enough to thread your piece of rope through.

4 *Following the method illustrated, lace the cord through the holes on the box and then pass the cord through the holes in the lid, so that the lid is securely laced to the box. Secure the ends with a double reef knot.*

5 *To decorate the box, secure flat found objects to the box with glue, steel wire or small nails. For example, you could glue a piece of beachcombed glass onto the front of the box or you could drill small holes in one or more sides of the box and lace wire through, using it to bind glass or found objects to the sides in a web effect.*

how to make a recycled necklace

Equipment and materials

Rope chain

String of graduated
fake pearls

String of small beads

Diamanté strand

Heart charm

12 small charms

Large crucifix

Box of brass jump rings

Medium spool of fine
brass wire

Round-nosed pliers

Wire cutters

This "recycled" necklace is very straightforward and need not be expensive to make. It involves binding existing jewellery pieces – either secondhand or new, but the feel should be "antique" – onto a chain to create a dazzling new necklace. The rope chain is the main ingredient for the design. Ieneke Boissevain has chosen a heavy, old-looking chain and has bound ready-assembled strings of beads onto it. To gauge the lengths you need, start by measuring your chosen rope chain. The bead lengths should be approximately half as long again to allow for winding around the rope, and the diamanté strand should be approximately half the length of the rope chain. Before you start winding the strings of beads onto the rope chain, remove the old clasps from the diamanté strand and from the two strings of beads that you are to bind around the rope chain (leave the clasp on the rope chain intact). Secure the unfinished ends of the bead strings by tying a double knot – this will prevent the beads from scattering everywhere once you start to wind them onto the rope chain.

Collect a good selection of bits and pieces from flea

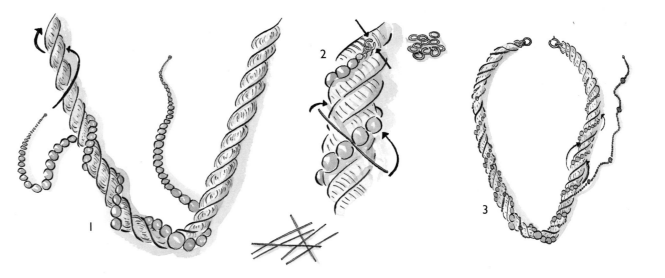

1 *With the rope chain on a work surface, lay the central point of the string of pearls over the central point of the chain. Starting at this point, begin to tightly wind the pearls around the chain. The pearls will naturally fall into the deep ridges which form the chain's rope-like structure. Continue in this way until the entire length of the pearl necklace is firmly wound around the chain.*

2 *Secure the string of pearls to the rope chain at 1- or 2-inch (2.5- or 5-cm) intervals by winding a length of fine brass wire (available from hardware stores) tightly and unobtrusively around both the chain and the string of pearl beads. Snip off*

the excess wire with wire cutters and carefully weave the wire ends back into the body of the rope chain to give a neat finish. Open two jump rings (see p.25) and attach one to each end of the string of pearl beads. To secure the ends of the fake pearl length to the main body of the necklace, fasten each jump ring to a corresponding link on either side of the rope chain, just in front of the clasp. Squeeze the joins in the jump rings tightly shut with round-nosed pliers.

3 *Attach a small string of beads – Ieneke Boissevain used a fine string of brass and coloured beads for her necklace, but you may prefer to use a length of brightly coloured rocaille beads –*

markets, boot or garage sales and thrift stores or charity shops. Top up your collection with charms and bead lengths bought from findings stores and craft catalogues. Ieneke Boissevain's selection of charms include anchors, seahorses, hearts and a dagger, but the style and number of charms you choose to decorate your necklace with will obviously depend on your own personal preference. Make sure that your chosen elements mix well in colour and for maximum impact consider working to a theme such as a religious, nautical or military look.

Previous pages: Discarded metal pieces are the main ingredient for (left to right) dangle earrings assembled from chains and stones; a dangle brooch incorporating wires from glasses; a brooch made from found media; and a silver-plated "sputnik" brooch.
(Michael de Nardo)

Right: This necklace is fashioned by twisting ready-made bead necklaces onto a brass rope chain. The two-tier effect is created by linking a short diamanté length to the inside of the rope chain. The necklace is then decorated with charms, trinkets and a crucifix.
(Ieneke Boissevain)

to the rope chain. Work in the same way as you did with the string of pearls, binding the beads in place with brass wire and securing the ends with jump rings.

4 *Thread the heart charm onto a jump ring and fix it to the middle of the diamanté length. Secure a jump ring to each end of the diamanté length. If the diamanté strand has no loop to which you can secure the jump rings, simply bind the jump rings with fine brass wire. Hook the jump rings onto a link on either side of the main rope chain. Squeeze the jump rings tightly shut with pliers. When attached, this second tier of the necklace should hang approximately 1in (2.5cm) above the*

middle point on the rope chain to which the crucifix will be attached.

5 *Embellish your completed necklace with an ornate crucifix and charms. Attach a jump ring to the crucifix and fasten this to the central point of the rope chain. Squeeze the join in the jump ring tightly shut with pliers. Thread each of the 12 small charms you have chosen to decorate the necklace with onto their own jump ring and link them onto the rope chain at intervals.*

You can also embellish the crucifix and the charms by attaching flat-backed cabochon-style stones, glitter and sequins with a suitable glue (see p.25).

artists & designers

Annaliese
available from Janet Fitch
Solid gold and silver jewellery.
See p. 114.

Antigona
217 rue Saint Honoré
75001 Paris, France
Costume jewellery. See p. 107.

Julie Arkell
46 Hornsey Rise
London N19 35Q
Jewellery made from found objects
and papier mâché. See p. 59.

Glynneth Barren
available from Janet Fitch
and from:
11360 Ovada Place
Suite 12, Los Angeles
California 90049, USA
Designs in paste, crystal, glass
and jet. See pp. 28, 32 & 80.

Eric Beamon
available from Janet Fitch
and from:
Showroom Seven
241 West 37th Street
12th Floor
New York 10018, USA
Crystal and suede tassel jew-
ellery. See pp. 34 & 38.

Ieneke Boissevain
available from Janet Fitch
Witty and original pieces made
from found objects. See p 136.

Barbara Bosha Nelson
Buspace Studio
Unit 17, Conlan Street
London W10 5AP
Jewellery crafted from natural
objects. See p. 101.

Bradley
Showroom Seven
241 West 37th Street
12th Floor
New York 10018, USA
Decorative enamelled
jewellery. See p. 33.

Victoria Brown
2nd Floor, Bombay Wharf
59 St. Mary Church Street
Rotherhithe SE16
Woollen bead jewellery.
See pp. 6, 69, 76 & 79.

Judy Clayton
64 Queens Road
Farnborough
Hampshire GU14 6DX
Machine-embroidered metal
jewellery. See pp. 68 & 72.

Emma Clegg
The Craft Centre and
Design Gallery
City Art Gallery
The Headrow
Leeds LS1 3AD
Knitted copper wire jewellery.
See p. 80.

Gill Clement
available from Janet Fitch
Decorative papier mâché
pieces. See pp. 58 & 61.

Chris Clyne
306 Fulham Road
London SW10 9ER
Fashion designer. See p. 20.

Julia Cook
available from Janet Fitch
New Baroque and fairytale
jewellery. See pp. 107,
111, 114 & 119.

Jenifer Corker
available from Janet Fitch
Jewellery designer specializing in
precious and non-precious metals.
See pp. 80, 95 & 106.

Simon Costin
54 Charterhouse Street
London EC1N 68A
Jewellery to commission.
See p. 17.

Caroline Coyne
available from Janet Fitch
Wire jewellery. See p. 8.

Jane Crawford
available from Janet Fitch
Metal and precious stone
jewellery. See p. 110.

Crowther and Sieff
available from Janet Fitch
Hand-crafted sterling-silver
jewellery. See p. 114.

Helen Davenport
available from Janet Fitch
Fashion jewellery combining
traditional and modern methods.
See p. 106.

Dinosaur Designs
available from Janet Fitch
Brightly coloured plastic jew-
ellery. See pp. 94 & 102.

Patrick Downing
see Karen Owens

Avrina Eggleston
The Portobello Trust
14 Conlan Street
London W10 5DB
Modern jewellery detailed with
gemstones and enamel.
See p. 106.

Marion Elliot
Unit 5, Coxpit Yard
Northington Street
London WC1N 2NP
Papier mâché jewellery.
See pp. 59 & 67.

Ruth Elliott
see Gail de Jong

Mary Farrell
Flat 10
2 Queenstown Road
Clapton E5 8NN
Coiled wire jewellery.
See pp. 6, 7, 81 & 86-87.

Julia Foster
available from Janet Fitch
Decorative metal jewellery,
including acid-etched designs.
See pp. 80 & 83.

Peter Foster
2 Grays Inn Residences
Clerkenwell Road
London EC1
Sculpted jewellery in silver and
broken glass. See p. 7.

Frannie
available from Janet Fitch
Hand-painted silk earrings and
cuff links. See p. 68.

Susie Freeman
71 Sheffield Terrace
London W8 7NB
Knitted jewellery incorporating
beads, shells and sequins.
See pp. 69 & 71.

Lil Gardner
available from Janet Fitch
Fun designs in plastics, acrylics
and resins. See pp. 5 & 95.

Lynette Garland
Wickstead House
13 County Street
London SE1
Paper and metal jewellery.
See pp. 58 & 63.

Janice Gilmore
Pageant Jewellery
28 Cyprus Park
Belfast BT5 6EA
Embroidered, hand-beaded
Byzantine and decorative art
jewellery. See p. 69.

Elizabeth Hainski
available from Janet Fitch
Specializes in gilding and
ceramics. See p. 117.

Holli Hallett-Sullivan
available from Janet Fitch
Specializes in papier mâché
jewellery, embellished with gold
leaf, mother of pearl and glass.
See pp. 2, 59 & 62.

Heart of the Woods
Jacqueline & Peter Ridley
13 Vayre Close
Chipping Sodbury
Bristol BS17 6NY
Hand-turned wooden jewellery.
See p. 49.

Sue Horth
see Outlaws Club
Metal mesh and fine wire
jewellery. See pp. 81 & 85.

Glenis Howshall
Flat 2, 36 West Street
Ashburton, Newton Abbott
Devon TQ13 7DU
Leather and fabric jewellery.
See p. 68.

Donna Louise Iredale
available from Janet Fitch
Slate, fossil and enamelled
jewellery. See p. 128.

Naomi James
45b Freegrove Road
London N7
Wooden jewellery. See p. 48.

Mark Jameson
see Outlaws Club
Ceramic jewellery. See p. 29.

Gail de Jong and
Ruth Elliott
102 Oxford Gardens
London W10
Sculpted fabric jewellery.
See pp. 68 & 74.

Jeannell Kolkman
Heemraadweg 703
1382 HC Weesp
The Netherlands
Papier mâché designs. See p. 58.

Laura Lee
available from Janet Fitch
Coloured acrylic jewellery.
See pp. 6 & 94.

Andrew Logan
The Glasshouse
Melior Place
London SE1 3QP
Sculptor working in glass and
mirror jewellery. See p. 44.

Alison MacCulloch
35 Stag Lane
Edgware, Middx HA8 5AG
Hand-carved marble and onyx
jewellery. See p. 114.

Sheila R. McDonald
Providence House
12 Gallants Lane
East Hurling
Norfolk NR16 2NQ
Enamel jewellery.
See pp. 106 & 107.

Tom McEwen
contact via Janet Fitch
Exciting jewellery incorporating
gemstones and precious metals.
See pp. 115 & 118.

Julia Manheim
4, Kingsgate Workshops
110-116 Kingsgate Road
London NW6 2JG
Paper sculpture.
See pp. 59 & 64.

Simon Milburn
21 Harewood Close
3 Bridges, Crawley, Sussex
Metal cutlery jewellery.
See pp. 124 & 125.

Linda Miller
available from Janet Fitch
Figurative machine-embroidered
jewellery. See p. 68.

Jane Morgan
available from Janet Fitch
Stained glass jewellery.
See pp. 28, 40-41 & 43.

Malcom Morris
available from Janet Fitch
Designer and maker of costume
jewellery. See p. 23.

Louise Nagle
available from Janet Fitch
Specializes in pewter and
enamel jewellery. See pp. 80,
107 & 113.

Michael de Nardo
available from Janet Fitch
Abstract designs incorporating
everyday objects. See pp. 68,
124 & 134.

Mandy Nash
Model House
Craft and Design Centre
Bull Ring
Llantrisant
Mid Glamorgan CF7 8ED
Contemporary designs, crafted
from aluminium and rubber.
See pp. 68 & 73.

Julie Nelson
available from Janet Fitch
Ceramic fossil jewellery
enclosed in steel.
See p. 144.

Maura Nicholson
available from Janet Fitch
Gold, copper and silver rings
and earrings incorporating
precious and semi-precious
stones. See p. 6.

Nieuwe Nomaden
Heemraadweg 703
1382 HC Weesp
The Netherlands
Specializes in jewellery crafted
from paper and recycled fabric.
See p. 58.

Bernard O'Reilly
available from Janet Fitch
Experimental and adventurous
jewellery. See p. 114.

Outlaws Club
49 Endell Street
London WC2H 9AG
Young, innovative jewellers.

Karen Owens & Patrick
Downing
available from Janet Fitch
Brightly coloured acrylic and
ceramic jewellery. See p. 28.

Rowena Park
see Outlaws Club
Acrylic jewellery. See p. 94.

Alex Raphael
30 Kensington Square
London W8 5HH
Enamel jewellery.
See pp. 106 & 109.

Ruth Ratner
available from Janet Fitch
Metal and glass costume
jewellery. See p. 28.

Simon Rees and Susan
Small
available from Janet Fitch
Specialize in electroforming
objects for jewellery.
See p. 114.

Eric Rhein
c/o Artwear
456 West Broadway
New York NY 10012
USA
Jewellery crafted from old
brocades. See p. 68.

Mercedes Robirosa
76 rue Dutot
76015 Paris, France
Costume jewellery. See p. 107.

Cynthia Rybakoff
c/o Fragments
107 Greene Street
New York NY 10012, USA
Specializes in wooden
jewellery. See p. 48.

Sheer Decadence
available from Janet Fitch
Jewellery incorporating metal,
fabric and beads.
See p. 69.

Daphne Shepherd
The Corner
Queen Street
Twyford, Nr. Winchester
Hampshire SO21 1QG
Necklaces and bracelets craft-
ed from natural horsehair.
See p. 68.

Annie Sherburne
Waterside Workshops
99 Rotherhithe Street
London SE16 4NF
Hand-crafted and -painted
wooden jewellery.
See pp. 7, 48, 55 & 56.

Louise Slater
205 Wandsworth
Workshop
86-96 Garratts Lane
London SW18 4DJ
Plastic and laminated jewellery.
See pp. 94, 98, 99, 115
& 122.

Susan Small
see Simon Rees

Hayley Smith
available from Janet Fitch
Hand-turned and -finished
wooden bangles.
See pp. 4, 48 & 52.

Kate Smith
46 Crompton Street
Derby DE1 1NX
Specializes in papier mâché
and laminated paper jewellery.
See p. 59.

Katrina Smith
5 Finaghy Park Central
Belfast BT10 0HP
Specializes in textile jewellery.
See p. 68.

Andrew Stoker
31 St James' Drive
London SW17 3RN
Intricate marbled paper and
origami jewellery.
See p. 19.

Hammine Tappenden
The Old Bakery
Locks Green
Porchfield
Isle of Wight
PO30 4PF
Laminated paper jewellery.
See p. 58.

Wilson Tontine
available from Janet Fitch
Designer of acrylic fashion
jewellery. See pp. 95 & 104.

Sam Ubhi
170 Tooting Bec Road
London SW17 8BH
Hand-made wooden bead and
metal jewellery. See p. 49.

Claire Underwood
available from Janet Fitch
Silver and enamel jewellery.
(Specializes in pendants.)
See p. 106.

Janet Van der Pol
available from Janet Fitch
Specializes in wire and crystal
earrings. See p. 95.

Van der Straeten
available from Janet Fitch
Specialize in large gold-plated
jewellery, including torques, in
Grecian styles.
See pp. 90, 92 & 120.

Carlo Giovanni Verda
Waterside Workshops
99 Rotherhithe Street
London SE16 4NF
Multi-media jewellery.
See p. 114.

Alexa Wilding
available from Janet Fitch
Intricate papier mâché
jewellery designs.
See p. 58.

Katherine Wilkins
12 Sigdon Road
London E8 1AP
Specializes in concrete and
wooden jewellery.
See pp. 129 & 132.

John Wind
Maximal Art
2131 North American
Street
Philadelphia PA 19122
U.S.A.
Found media jewellery.
See pp. 6, 125 & 127.

Yukatek
c/o Fredric Pidancet
13 rue Stephenson
750017 Paris
France
Twisted wire and cork
jewellery. See pp. 28, 48, 81
& 84.

directory

United Kingdom Suppliers

Acrylic Designs
697 Harrow Road
London NW10 5NY
Plastic manufacturers.

Alma (London) Ltd
12-14 Greatorex Street
London E1 5NF
Leather suppliers.

Amari Plastics
2 Cumberland Avenue
North, Park Royal
London NW10 7RL
Plastic suppliers.

Bead Shop
43 Neal Street East
London WC2H 9PJ
Beads, findings and synthetic modelling clay. Also mail order and wholesale service.

Linda Bee
Stand J20/21
Grays Antique Market
1-7 Davies Mews
London W1Y 1AR
Art Deco jewellery supplier.

Brighton Bead Shop
21 Sydney Street
Brighton, Sussex BN1 4EN
Bone, pearl, ebony, shell, pewter, plastic, ceramic, wooden and metal beads. Also mail order service.

By the Yard
14 Berwick Street
London W1V 3RF
Fabric suppliers. Also mail order service.

Capital Gems
30b Great Sutton Street
London EC1V 0DU
Precious and semi-precious beads. Also mail order service.

Chelsea Glass
650 Portslade Road
London SW8 3DJ
Glass suppliers.

Cobra & Bellamy
149 Sloane Street
London SW1
Decorative art and 20th-century jewellery.

Janet Coles Beads Ltd
Perdiswell Cottage
Bilford Road
Worcester WR3 8QA
Large selection of beads, findings and bead kits. Also jewellery-making service.

L. Cornelissen & Son Ltd
105 Russell Street
London WC1
Fine artist materials.

Crispins
92-96 Curtain Road
London EC2A 3AA
Wood veneer suppliers.

R. Denny & Co. Ltd
13 Netherwood Road
London W14 0BL
Plastics suppliers, including Perspex and acrylic.

Dryad Press
P.O. Box 38
Northgate
Leicester LE1 4QR
Suppliers of kilns, enamelling materials and equipment, jewellery findings, general jeweller's tools, adhesives and polishes.

Elliot-Fitzpatrick
31 Hatton Garden
London EC1 8DH
Professional gilders.

Ells and Farrier Ltd
20 Beak Street
London W1R 3HA
Suppliers of beads, findings, stones, embroidery materials and sequins.

Exchange Findings Ltd
11-13 Hatton Wall
London EC1N 8HX
Suppliers of precious metals, findings and jeweller's equipment.

Faustus Fine Arts
90 Jermyn Street
London W1
Wearable ancient-gold jewellery.

Janet Fitch
2 Percy Street
London W1P 9FA
and
25 Old Compton Street
London W1V 5PL
*The **Janet Fitch** shops have established themselves as showcases for the work of contemporary designers of jewellery, fashion accessories and decorative objects. A successful launch-pad for art students, craftsmen and designers, they sell an eclectic mixture of exciting and innovative designs by new and established designers.*

Frontiers
39 Pembridge Road
London W11 3HG
Semi-precious stones, ethnic, antique and tribal jewellery.

Fulham Pottery
8-10 Ingate Place
London SW8 3NS
Ceramic suppliers.

Gunham Plastics Ltd
40 Rivington Street
London EC2A 3LX
Plastics suppliers.

Hamar Acrylic Fabrication Ltd
49 Bethnal Green Road
London E1 6LA
Plastic suppliers and manufacturers.

Hobby Horse
11 Blue Boar Street
Oxford OX1 4EZ
Beads and findings.

R. Holt and Co. Ltd
98 Hatton Gardens
London EC1N 8NX
Precious and semi-precious beads. Also mail order service.

John Jesse
160 Kensington Church Street
London W8 4BN
20th-century decorative arts.

John Lewis Partnership
278-306 Oxford Street
London W1
Fabric suppliers. Also ribbons, beads and sequins.

Kaleidoscope Crafts
3 Grove Park
Brislington
Bristol BS4 3LG
Beads and jewellery findings. Also mail order service.

Kall Kwick
106 Pembroke Road
Ruislip, Middx HA4 8NW
Laminated paper suppliers. (200 branches nationwide.)

Kenneth Jay Lane
30 Burlington Arcade
London W1V 9AD
Costume jewellery.

Lead and Light
34a Hartland Road
London NW1 4DB
Stained glass suppliers. Also mail order service.

Levy Gems Company Ltd
57 Hatton Garden
London EC1N 8HU
Precious and semi-precious beads and stones. Also mail order service.

Liberty & Co. Ltd
210 Regent Street
London W1
Large selection of ethnic and contemporary jewellery.
See pp. 12-13.

The London Bead Company
25 Chalk Farm Road
London NW1 8AG
Seed beads, sequins, crystals and findings.

Marcus McCallum
3rd Floor
The London Diamond Club
87 Hatton Garden
London EC1N 8QQ
Precious and semi-precious beads.

Marchmade Ltd
79 Dean Stret
London W1
Perspex and acrylic suppliers.

The Necklace Maker Workshop
259 Portobello Road
London W11 1LR
Exotic, antique and collectable beads. Beadwork, findings and threads. Commissions and repairs undertaken. Threading tuition. (No mail order.)

Pentonville Rubber Co. Ltd
50 Pentonville Road
London N1 9HF
Rubber suppliers.

Madeleine C. Popper
L12/13 Grays in the Mews
1-7 Davies Street
London W1Y 1AR
Antique jewellery.

Pottery Crafts
75 Silver Street
Edmonton
London N18 1RP
Ceramic suppliers. Also mail order service.

Poyner and Weatherley Ltd
The Stoneyard
Dorset Road
London N15
Marble suppliers.

Print Fast
24 Rathbone Place
London W1P 1DG
Laminated paper suppliers.

Mary Quant
3 Ives Street
London SW3 2NE
High fashion costume jewellery.

George Rowney & Co. Ltd.
12 Percy Street
London W1A 2BP
Artist materials. Also suppliers of synthetic modelling clay.

Stained Glass Suppliers
41-49 Kingsland Road
London E2 8AD
Suppliers of stained glass. (Mail order service available.)

Steinberg & Tolkien
183 Kings Road
Chelsea
London SW3 5EB
Period costume jewellery (c. 1900-1960).

Alex Tiranti
27 Warren Street
London W1P 5DG
Large selection of jeweller's tools and equipment for modelling, carving and casting. Supplier of pewter, acrylic paints and gold leaf. Gilding undertaken.

Travis Perkins
13 St. Pancras Way
London NW1 9PJ
Wood suppliers.

H.S. & C.S. Walsh Ltd
12-16 Clerkenwell Road
London EC1
Jeweller's tools, findings and enamelling equipment and materials.

Westbrook and Thompson Ltd
30 Newington Causeway
London SE1
Rubber suppliers.

Katy Williams
c/o **Pars Antiques**
Stand A14/15
Grays in the Mews
1-7 Davies Street
London W1Y 1AR
Classical, Persian and Islamic antiquities and jewellery.

Peter H. Wolfe & Gudde
c/o Jane Skyrme Workshops
84 Camden Mews
London NW1 9BX
Suppliers of enamelling equipment and materials. Also mail order service.

Museums

British Museum
Great Russell Street
Bloomsbury, London WC1
Roman, Etruscan, Greek and Cypriot, Anglo Saxon, Byzantine, Medieval, Renaissance and Victorian jewellery collections on display.

Museum of Mankind
6 Burlington Gardens
London W1
Ethnic jewellery collections, including 1900s gold bracelets from Zanzibar, Ashanti gold discs and torques.

Pitt Rivers Museum
South Park Road
Oxford OX1 3PP
Large collection of ethnic jewellery, including North African beadwork, Tuareg, Naga Indian, Amazonian, North American and Roman jewellery.

Victoria and Albert Museum
Cromwell Road
London SW7 2RL
Jewellery dating from 300AD to present day. Includes Egyptian, Etruscan, Byzantine, Medieval, Pre-Columbian and 17th-, 18th- and 19th-century collections. Also 1940s, 1950s, Trifari, Boucher and 1960s-1980s costume jewellery.

North American Suppliers

All Craft Tool and Supply Company, Inc.
3rd Floor
45 West 46th Street
New York NY 11217
Jewelry materials and tools, including enameling equipment.

All Craft Tool and Supply Company, Inc.
666 Pacific Street, Brooklyn, New York 11217
Jewelry equipment. Mail order.

Art to wear
4202 Water Oaks Lane
Tampa, Florida 33624
Beads, tools, findings and manuals. Also mail order.

Beads Galore International, Inc.
2123 South Priest
Suite #201
Tempe, Arizona 85282
Semi-precious stones, wooden beads, brass beads, folk-art beads, pearls, charms and findings. Also mail order.

Beadworks
139 Washington Street
South Norwalk
Connecticut 06854
and:
905 South Ann Street
Baltimore, Maryland 21231
Beads, findings, accessories and books. Also mail order.

The Clay Factory of Escondido
P.O. Box 460598
Escondido
California 92046-0598
Suppliers of jewelry tools, equipment, findings and modeling clay. Also mail order.

Gypsy Wind
147 Sacremento Street
Auburn CA 95603
Wide range of glass, crystal and metal beads. Also precious and semi-precious stones, pearls, metal stampings, findings and stringing materials. Threading tuition undertaken.

Handy and Harman
250 Park Avenue
New York NY 10017
Precious metal and tubing suppliers.

Industrial Plastics
309 Canal Street
New York NY 10013
Plastics suppliers, including resins, dyes and adhesives.

International Bead and Jewelry Supply
2368 Kettner Blvd.
San Diego CA 92101
Large range of exotic hand-fashioned beads from around the world.

Kuma Company
Dept. Y
P.O. Box 2719
Glenville
New York NY 12325
Suppliers of jeweler's tools, materials and equipment, gemstones, findings, fittings and a wide selection of reference books.

glossary

Alum A proprietary pickling solution, which is non-toxic and safe to use.

Alumina An oxide of aluminium used for making synthetic stones in different colours.

Amulet A protective charm, believed to ward off evil spirits and illness.

Anneal The process of heating and cooling metal in order to soften it and prevent it from cracking.

Bakelite The first synthetic plastic to be invented. A heat-resistant substance that does not soften when it is heated.

Base metal A non-precious metal, ie. copper, iron, aluminium, nickel and brass.

Bell cap A decorative metal finding which is attached to a necklace fastening to conceal the multiple threads.

Blow pipe A brass tube which is tapered at one end and connected to a rubber tubing mouthpiece at the other. It is used for achieving a fine flame for soldering.

Buff stick A wooden rod covered with sandpaper or emery paper, used to smooth an object before polishing.

Bull stick A graving tool which is used to cut the ledge (bearer) on which a stone rests in its setting.

Cameo A jewel that is decorated with a carved design (often a figure) in low relief.

Crucible An earthenware container used for holding molten metals.

Deoxidizer A solution of sulphuric acid and water which is used to remove the oxide which builds up on precious metals during soldering.

Diamanté Rhinestones or any non-precious stones that have the appearance and brilliance of diamonds.

Diamond grit An abrasive used for cutting diamonds.

Electrogilding A method of gilding metal by depositing a thin layer of 24 carat gold to its surface. The process replaced gilding using mercury, which was considered to be too dangerous, but is prone to wear away quickly.

Electroplating The process of coating an object with a thin layer of metal by means of a small electrical current.

Email en ronde bosse Encrused enamelling.

Facet The flat angled surface or face of a cut gemstone.

Faience A fired ground quartzite combined with an oxide to create a coloured pigmentation.

Filigree Fine wire, usually gold or silver, which is used decoratively. It can be soldered to a metal base or backed – without a base it is called openwork.

Findings Small, mass-produced components common to many different types of jewellery, eg. catches, clasps and fittings (see p.26).

Fire stain The black staining that occurs on silver when it is heated. (Copper contained in the impure silver reacts to oxygen in the air.)

Firing fork A long stainless steel implement used for placing objects in, and removing them from, a kiln.

Fretsaw A deep-bladed saw used for cutting plywood.

Gilding A mixture of mercury and gold dust which is applied to a surface. Once the mercury has evaporated, a thin layer of gold is left.

Gold leaf An expensive, wafer-thin material used for gilding non-metallic objects. It is obtained in booklets in a range of sizes and thicknesses and is applied by hand.

Gold paint A liquid, gold-coloured paint which is obtained in bottles from art supply stores.

Gouache paint An opaque water-based paint.

Granulated A metal surface covered with small elevations.

Hallmark An impression stamped on gold, silver or platinum items which guarantees the purity of that metal.

Ingot A slab of cast metal particularly gold, silver or steel.

Jasparware A hard, finely grained, unglazed stoneware created by Josiah Wedgwood. It is predominantly blue with a white relief design, similar to that of a cameo.

Lapidary A craftsperson who prepares, cuts, engraves and polishes gemstones.

Lapis lazuli A gemstone made up of various blue-coloured minerals with a dull lustre that can be polished.

Lathkin roller A wooden roller with a handle which is used to press the edges of copper foil onto glass.

Millefiori An Italian term meaning a "thousand flowers". Ornamental glass, made by fusing canes of coloured glass together, often used for enamelling and glass work.

Panning mesh A metal grille which is used to support a piece, eg. an enamel disc, in the kiln.

Paste Glass of varying types used to simulate gemstones.

Pavé set A style of stone setting whereby numerous small gemstones are set very close together in order to cover the metal in a paved decoration.

Piercing saw A saw with a very narrow blade which is threaded through a drilled hole so as to create a design.

Plywood Manmade wooden boarding made from thin layers of wood which are glued together in a sandwich-effect.

Powdered oxide A basic refactory used in the creation of synthetic stones.

Pumice An abrasive material of porous lava which is used, in either stone or powder form, in the finishing stages of metal and enamel.

Repoussé A technique in which the reverse side of a metal is punched to create a relief design on the front.

Rocaille A tiny glass bead that is used for jewellery-making, beadweaving and embroidery.

Rose-cut A method of cutting gemstones to produce a flat-based stone with many small facets rising to a low point.

Rouge A fine abrasive material of red iron oxide which is used to polish precious metals and stones.

Sand blasting A technique, often carried out after casting, which involves directing a jet of sand onto the surface of an object to achieve a matte finish.

Scriber A sharp steel rod which is used for marking lines on wood, metal or glass which are to be cut or drilled.

Shearing A method of cutting sheet metal, using specialist cutting shears.

Suite (or parure) A set of jewellery decorated with the same variety of gemstone ie. a diamond necklace and earrings worn as a set.

Talisman Similar to an amulet, but with an emphasis on the object possessing magical and astrological properties.

Torque (torch or tore) A metal neck ring or armlet with a back opening – usually of Celtic origin.

Tripoli An abrasive material used for polishing metal.

Zoomorphic Representing animals in art.

index

acknowledgments

Janet Fitch would like to thank:

My family for their understanding; Martin Somervail, from the Janet Fitch shop, for his invaluable help and humour; Shirley Conran for her friendship and for getting me started in the first place; Jonathan Kernan, Lisa Brinkworth and Ben Lewis for their help in researching the book; Patrick Newell for his support and inspiration; Stephen Mahoney for his help and support and for lending ethnic jewellery; Paul Stone, my partner at Stone Design Associates, for his forebearance; David Crottie, Chris and Craig for keeping a (reluctant) me fit; Joyce Bennett, Manuela Gomez and Jenny Powell for keeping the home fires burning; Zoe Reed, Joyce Kauffeld and Jane Platford for typing; Stefany Tomalin, from the Necklace Maker (and author of the Bead Book), for her patience, help and advice on the subject; Peter Page, goldsmith (4, The Square, Ramsbury, Marlborough, Wiltshire), for his help with the metal chapter; Gudde Jane Skyrme, from the British Society of Enamellers, for her help with the enamel chapter; and to all my friends who've cheered me along.

Thanks are also due to the following for lending jewellery for the history and ethnic pictures: John Jesse for the loan of the Lalique brooch; Madeleine C. Popper for the shawl pin, human hair brooch, jet earrings, ironwork and pinchbeck necklaces; Linda Bee for the bakelite brooch; Cobra and Bellamy for the Chanel necklace; Steinberg and Tolkein for the Schiaparelli set; Faustus Fine Art for the ancient Roman ring; Nicola Clark for the Pam Hogg heart pendant, eye ring, Christian Lacroix pendant and cuff; Mary Quant for the daisy earring; Simon Costin for the rabbit skull brooch; Pars Antiques for the faience necklace; Kenneth J. Lane for the panther brooch; Liberty & Co. Ltd for the Billy Boy jewellery, Tibetan necklace, Chinese combs, African beads, Ethiopian necklace, Mexican earrings, Indian bracelet, Moroccan bangle, Egyptian beads and Indian ring; and the Museum of London for the replica pilgrim's brooch.

Thank you to Judith More, Jacqui Small, Catherine Smith and Trinity Fry for being so good to work with and for their guidance. And finally, thank you to all the designers in this book – a big thank you for lending their work, but most of all for being creative and good to know – this is their book.

Mitchell Beazley would like to thank Sara Morris and Cameron Watt for assisting with the photography.

Right: You can bind wire around found objects to produce original items of personalized jewellery. The graphite-coloured ceramic components of this fish-shaped earring are secured by binding them with galvanized steel wire — the twised fish hook adds a quirky finishing touch. (Julie Nelson)